POLISH HEADS

OF

HOUSEHOLD

IN

MARYLAND

An Index to the
1910 Census

Thomas L. Hollowak

HERITAGE BOOKS
2012

HERITAGE BOOKS

AN IMPRINT OF HERITAGE BOOKS, INC.

Books, CDs, and more—Worldwide

For our listing of thousands of titles see our website
at
www.HeritageBooks.com

Published 2012 by
HERITAGE BOOKS, INC.
Publishing Division
100 Railroad Ave. #104
Westminster, Maryland 21157

Originally Published: 1990

Other Heritage Books by Thomas L. Hollowak:

Longevity List of Baltimore City, 1880–1889: An Index to the List of Decedents, Aged 70 Years and Upwards Appearing in Annual Reports of the Board of Health, Baltimore City

International Standard Book Numbers
Paperbound: 978-1-58549-179-7
Clothbound: 978-0-7884-9171-9

INDEX TO THE POLISH HEADS-OF-HOUSEHOLD
IN THE 1910 CENSUS FOR MARYLAND

Baltimore served as an important port of entry for large
numbers of Polish immigrants after the American Civil War. Most
of them continued on to midwestern cities and rural communities.
In 1868 a small number of these immigrants began to settle in the
city. Arriving at Locust Point those who chose to stay crossed
the harbor and took up residence in Fell's Point.

In 1870 there were approximately ten Polish families in
Baltimore, many of them living in close proximity to one another.
As the number of families increased so did their geographical
distribution. Although they continued to settle primarily in
Fell's Point economic opportunies in Canton and Baltimore County
to the east and across the harbor in Anne Arundel County led to
Polish settlements in those areas. However, except for those
engaged in migrant farm work, Poles were not to be found outside
Baltimore City and these two counties.

The 1910 Census

The 1910 Census is an important aid to researchers for
several reasons. First, it is the last census taken before World
War I (which began in 1914 in Europe and effectively stopped
large-scale Polish immigration to America). Second, it was the
first census to recognize the partitioning of Poland. As a
result the place of birth of immigrants or the native-born
children of immigrants enumerated indicates the partitioned area
(i.e. German Poland, Austrian Poland, or Russian Poland).

Finally, the occupation category is less vague by addressing two questions: Trade or profession? and Nature of business? To understand the importance of this one must recall prior censuses which listed simply "laborer" as the individual's occupation. In the 1910 census the individual who gave "laborer" also provided additional information on the type of laborer he was. For example the response could range from "coal pier to odd jobs."

The 1910 census like those which came before it provides other valuable information about birth, marriage, death, familial relationships, education, home ownership, immigration, and naturalization. The lack of either an index or soundex leads to difficulty in gaining access to this information. The index that follows will solve this problem.

The Index

The heads-of-household, boarders, in-laws, and other relatives with a diffrent surname than the head-of-household are included in this index. Arranged alphabetically by surname, the index also provides county, enumeration district, and the page where the individual can be found in the census. The 3,671 individuals cited were living in Baltimore City (Wards 1, 2, and 3) and Anne Arundel and Baltimore counties. In 1918 Baltimore City annexed many of the areas were the Poles lived in these two counties (i.e. Brooklyn, Curtis Bay, Locust Point, and Wagner's Point in Anne Arundel county; and Caton, as well as, along the Belair and Harford roads in Baltimore County).

Using the Index

The researcher using this index should be aware of a few quirks that may cause initial difficulty in locating a particular individual. The computer program used in compiling this index did not allow for modification of the format after information had been entered. As a result some of the three-digit enumeration districts had to be accommodated under the page listing. To ease this problem a table has been provided of all enumeration districts and their appropriate ward or district (see Table 1). The abreviations used are as follows: CO = county, ED = enumeration district, and PAG = page.

TABLE 1

County/City	E. D.	Ward or District
Anne Arundel	5	Dist. 2
	7-9	Dist. 3
	12-14	Dist. 4
	15-16	Dist. 5
	17	Dist. 2/5
	18	Dist. 5
	19/21	Annapolis
Baltimore City	1-14	Ward 1
	15-25	Ward 2
	26	Ward 3
	35-90	Ward 3
	109	Ward 3
	141-142	Ward 3
	146	Ward 3
	243	Ward 3
	406	Ward 2
Baltimore County	7	Dist. 1-2
	31	Dist. 9
	39	Dist. 11
	41-51	Dist. 12
	53-55	Dist. 13
	58	Dist. 14
	65-66	Dist. 15
	68	Dist. 13/15

Acknowlegments

As part of the research needed for my masters thesis I hired Jeanne S. Davis to compile a listing of all Polish immigrants and those individuals of Polish ancestry in Maryland. This index has been compiled from the data she provided.

Over the last ten years I have been compiling information on all aspects of Polish immigrant life in Baltimore. The data gathered as a result is a formitable resource useful to genealogists. I am willing to share the genealogical gleanings for a modest fee of $25.00. Anyone interested should write me c/o: Family Line Publications, Rear 63 E. Main Street, Westminster, Maryland 21157.

Thomas L. Hollowak
Baltimore   July 1990

THE INDEX

Last	First	CO	ED	PAG
Abreinski	Konstanty	BA	9	2
Adamikewich	Adam	AA	18	6b
Adamoscky	John	BA	8	9
Adamska	Katerzyna	BA	40	612
Adamski	Frank	BA	18	16
Adamski	John	BA	26	3
Adamski	Joseph	BA	8	10
Aeglowith	Joseph	BA	19	11
Agustajmowics	Enacy	BA	8	4
Ainkowicz	Alexander	BA	17	26
Aipen	Francis	BA	19	35
Alexalzer	Ludwich	AA	18	2
Alexanderowicz	Stanislaw	BA	40	612
Alexanza	Konstantin	AA	18	3
Ambros	Boleslaw	BA	40	612
Anastasia	Mary, Sister	BA	17	17
Andeyak	Agnizka	BA	40	6 6
Andjeska	John	BA	8	14
Andrchoski	Antonie	BA	17	31
Andresejeski	Sophia	BA	8	11
Andrew	Frank	BA	16	7
Andrew	Martin	BA	5	22
Andreyewski	Stanislaus	BA	25	7
Andrisski	Stoneslauce	AA	17	11
Andrysiak	Walenty	BA	19	30
Andryziak	Joseph	BA	19	17
Andrzack	Joseph	AA	18	9
Andrzeyewski	Felix	BA	16	4
Andrzeyewski	Felix W.	BA	16	4
Andrzeyewski	Frank	BA	14	2
Andrzjieruski	John	AA	13	12
Andrzyziak	John	BA	19	17
Andzyszek	Andrey F.	BA	19	28
Anna	Sister	BA	17	17
Annsrewski	Joseph	BA	8	7
Ant	Michael	BA	18	9
Antkowiak	John	BA	9	2
Antkowiak	Martin J.	BA	10	20
Antkowski	John	BA	9	1
Antonziewski	Josef	BA	19	34
Antowiak	Allan	BA	26	7
Antryska	Edward	BA	9	4
Anuszewski	Andrew	BA	19	2
Anuzewski	Michel	BA	15	6
Arcowski	Frank	BA	25	17
Arendt	Michael	BA	16	4
Arka	Francis	BA	22	15
Arscyowski	Antonie	BA	21	10
Artha	Michael	BA	22	7
Arzechowski	Lorenz	BA	19	10

Last	First	CO	ED	PAG
Asculoski	Walinti	BA	26	15
Asmalak	Mary	BA	19	11
Astinewski	Andrew	BA	19	20
Augustiniak	Valentin	BA	40	6 8
Augustiniuk	Joseph	BA	40	6 4
Augustinyak	John J.	BA	23	15
Augustuski	Frank	BA	19	9
Augustyniak	Michael	BA	19	10
Augustyniski	Masim	BA	19	26
Augustynowska	Eva	BA	17	5
Bachenski	Jacob	BA	17	19
Bachenski	Martin	BA	17	17
Back	Kasimerz	BA	24	11
Backlinski	John	AA	8	2
Baczak	Franciszek	BA	15	13
Badelfyak	Simon	BA	26	13
Bagensky	Alexander	BA	40	6 2
Baginski	John	BA	17	18
Bagrowski	Joseph	BA	3	21
Baker	Paul	BA	22	16
Baker	Stephen	BA	26	8
Bakowski	George	BA	22	11
Balcera	Martin	BA	19	1
Balcerowic	Walter	BA	18	8
Balcerowicz	Czeslaw	BA	18	13
Balczerowski	Andrew	BA	17	31
Baliga	Rosia	BA	18	6
Balinski	Antoniatt	BA	19	14
Balis	Michael	BA	5	14
Balowitski	Thoman	BA	5	22
Balster	Helen	BA	17	25
Bamer	Frank	BA	2	13
Banashak	George	BA	5	14
Banasjewski	Joe	BA	1	14
Bandorska	Victoria	BA	8	8
Bandzwol	Joseph	BA	3	21
Banzdzicnck	Stanislas	BA	3	8
Barabsz	Weczlaus	BA	35	18
Baranoski	Jacob	BA	8	6
Baranoski	John	BA	19	11
Baranoski	Martin	BA	19	11
Baranowski	Alexander	BA	17	6
Baranowski	Francis	BA	18	6
Baranowski	Max	BA	8	11
Baraswerke	Frank	BA	1	7
Barbinski	Heriman	BA	19	14
Barcrak	Andres	BA	19	4
Baresek	Francis	BA	8	6
Barke	John	BA	26	12
Barnowski	Joseph	AA	13	17b

Last	First	CO	ED	PAG
Barohn	Mary	BA	19	11
Barowski	Stanislaus	BA	8	4
Barrajyucki	Ramazki	BA	19	11
Barranouski	Leona	BA	19	11
Barron	James	BA	19	6
Barrufskie	Andrew	AA	17	9a
Barryk	Peter	BA	26	9
Bartecki	Thomas	BA	17	13
Bartkowak	Michael	BA	19	5
Bartkowiak	Frank	BA	8	5
Bartkowiak	Henry	BA	8	11
Bartkowiak	Stanley F.	BA	8	11
Bartkowska	Mary	BA	22	15
Bartkowski	Frank	BA	11	9
Bartkowski	Martin	BA	17	35
Bartok	Stanislow	AA	18	6b
Bartonewicz	John	BA	17	5
Bartoss	Franciscek J.	BA	19	24
Bartow	William H.	BA	19	28
Bartowiak	Stanislaus	BA	1	18
Barylski	Michael	BA	19	16
Batotsky	Lawrance	AA	18	9
Batster	John	BA	17	29
Bausch	Bronislaus	BA	19	11
Bauzak	Michael	BA	26	8
Bawasgak	Constantia	BA	14	14
Baxansky	Raymond	AA	18	11
Baykoski	Mary	BA	11	3
Bazkowski	Joseph	BA	17	35
Bearliskie	Wadislouce	AA	17	13b
Bebinski	Joseph	BA	19	29
Becniak	Maggie	BA	26	14
Bedura	Shidurer	BA	26	5
Befiony	Frank	BA	17	19
Begier	Mary	BA	19	29
Bejlski	Michel	BA	15	7
Bejoma	Stanislau	BA	1	13
Bekczynki	Adam	BA	18	3
Bekowski	Jan J.	BA	17	27
Belair	Michael	BA	8	9
Beldys	Andrew	BA	17	19
Beling	John	BA	19	5
Belinski	Joseph	BA	3	2
Beliski	Stephen	BA	19	22
Belkowski	Henry	BA	11	3
Bender	Joseph	BA	10	9 4
Benelski	Petin	BA	18	18
Bengies	Andrew	BC	48	15
Benhoff	Steven	BA	2	13
Beniseska	Maryanna	BA	4	1

4

Last	First	CO	ED	PAG
Bennett	John	BA	17	30
Bennett	Michael	BA	17	30
Bennotski	Annie	BA	18	13
Beozkowski	Joseph	BA	17	29
Berdych	Mary	AA	14	6a
Bernadzikowski	Frank	BA	9	5
Berrent	Alexander	BA	3	10
Beser	Francis	BA	8	11
Betka	Frank	BA	16	5
Bettejewski	John	BA	9	24
Bettejewski	Joseph	BA	18	15
Bettejewski	Marian	BA	18	15
Beyick	Paul	BA	19	18
Bezkia	Frank	BA	26	10
Bialecki	Jan	BA	2	13
Bialek	Joseph	BA	40	6 5
Bialek	Joseph L.	BA	5	12
Bialek	Marga	BA	18	2
Bialek	Michael	BA	3	2
Bialek	Paul	BA	9	5
Bialobrzesky	Frank	BA	40	610
Bialosinski	Louis	BA	8	6
Bialosinski	Michael	BA	8	6
Bialozynska	Josephine	BA	8	6
Bialozynska	William	BA	8	6
Bibik	Adela	BA	17	15
Bichno	Stanislaus	BA	17	15
Biczuk	Peter	BA	40	6 8
Biedronski	Frank	BA	16	1
Biedrzyski	Vincent	BA	17	3
Bielat	Marcas	BA	16	2
Bien	Robert	BA	9	24
Bienert	Theodore	BA	15	7
Bienkowski	Anthony	BA	3	20
Bienkowski	Joseph	BA	3	20
Biernacki	Antonia	BA	11	7
Bietanetay	Anna	BA	35	22
Binczkowski	Felix	BA	17	18
Bindinenski	Henry	BA	17	25
Binke	Adam	BA	16	9
Binkowski	Emile	BA	3	9
Binkowsky	Michael	BA	40	6 7
Bint	Michael	BA	15	10
Binzkoski	Joseph	BA	26	6
Biolozyaiski	John	BA	8	4
Biskupski	Frank	BA	24	1
Biskupski	Theodore	BA	19	23
Bistrick	Anna	BA	40	6 4
Blachomez	Rosie	BA	40	613
Blanle	George	BA	26	12

Last	First	CO	ED	PAG
Blarkowski	Marryanna	BA	15	12
Blasack	Joseph	BA	4	2
Blaszezak	Nichlas	BA	22	12
Bleja	John	BA	1	14
Blochowiz	John	BA	40	610
Block	John	BA	40	613
Blusewicz	Alexander	BA	17	37
Bluzczyk	Leokadza	BA	35	17
Boajanowski	Franz	BC	48	10
Bobel	Frank	BA	18	22
Bober	Edward	BA	2	6
Bober	Walter	BA	1	15
Bochenski	Albert	BA	15	13
Bochenski	Joseph	BA	26	5
Bochiak	Kazmer	BA	40	6 2
Bochinski	Frank	BA	17	25
Bochynck	Joseph	BA	18	10
Bocks	Andrew	BA	18	10
Bodnick	Dora	BA	18	16
Bodski	Francis	BA	19	3
Bogaciewicz	Maryanna	BA	18	19
Bogdan	Michael	BA	26	5
Bogdanweisch	Adam	BA	5	22
Bogdinowicz	Julia	BA	26	14
Bogdon	John	BC	48	15
Bogenski	Alexander	BA	19	18
Bogzomsky	Michael	BA	40	6 4
Bohowich	Joseph	BA	26	4
Bojansky	Wojciech	BA	40	6 5
Bojkowski	Adam	BA	17	18
Bokowski	Stephen	BA	19	33
Boldwinski	Joseph	BA	11	6
Boldwinski	Ojoneck	BA	11	6
Boleski	Ignatus	BA	19	20
Bolesky	Antony	BC	41	112
Bolewczynski	Alexander	BA	18	8
Bolewick	John	BA	19	7
Bolewicski	James	BA	8	7
Bolewinsky	Michael	BA	1	14
Bolser	Georges	BA	40	6 6
Bolski	Julian	BA	19	14
Bomkosski	Andrew	BA	3	20
Bonaszewski	Andrew	BA	1	17
Bonaszewski	John	BA	1	16
Bonchek	Anton	BA	15	13
Boney	Steve	AA	14	6a
Bonsrewicz	Pawel	BA	17	28
Bontkowski	Frank	BA	15	13
Bonzowiak	John	BA	8	7
Boracki	Martin	BA	13	9

Last	First	CO	ED	PAG
Borasi	Ausilu	BA	19	5
Borazki	Frank	BA	16	4
Borchowicz	Jim	BA	40	6 8
Borchowski	John	BA	26	9
Borczynsky	Pawel	BA	40	610
Boresvski	Martin	BA	17	33
Boreszki	Jacob	BA	17	32
Boriniskie	Stonestonce	AA	17	12a
Borkowski	Alex	BA	19	5
Borkowski	Francis	BA	19	16
Borkowski	John	BC	3	13
Borkowski	Joseph	BA	19	16
Borodia	Anuffer	AA	18	2
Boromic	Andreas	BA	40	6 2
Borowicz	Alexander	BA	18	21
Borowski	John	BA	18	10
Borowski	Peter	BA	19	6
Borowski	Stanislai	BA	1	13
Boroziak	Walter	BA	18	14
Bortusskensur	Vincent	BA	35	11
Borzt	Adam	BA	17	35
Boskopfsky	Joseph	BC	68	29
Boskoski	John	BA	21	3
Boskowski	Felix	BA	23	15
Bosozowska	Julia	BA	10	11
Bourchyki	Andy	BA	19	26
Bowkoski	Andrew	BA	21	3
Box	Jesophat	BA	19	12
Boyer	John	BA	9	6
Bozokowski	John	BA	18	5
Bozonofski	Frank	AA	16	1b
Bozuchowski	Julian J.	BA	18	5
Bozuzki	William	BA	1	12
Brachnicki	John	BA	17	26
Bradowsky	Adam	BC	48	15
Brakeneczka	Joseph	BA	17	17
Bram	John	BA	18	22
Brawski	Frank	BA	17	5
Brazinsky	John	AA	18	3
Breckels	Josephine	BA	2	10
Breczke	Felix	BA	17	1
Breda	Kenba	BA	19	32
Brenskie	Julius	BA	9	12
Bresinski	Michael	BA	17	19
Brikowski	Mary	BA	17	17
Brink	John H.	BA	3	9
Brink	Rose	BA	19	34
Brochauski	August	BA	19	22
Brochewisno	Michel	BA	16	4
Brocinskey	Joseph	AA	17	4b

Last	First	CO	ED	PAG	
Brocki	Michael	BA	16	4	
Brocky	William	BA	40	6	4
Brocosske	Julian	BA	26	19	
Broczkowski	Juljan	BA	17	8	
Broczkowsky	Antonie	BA	40	613	
Broda	Stephan	BA	15	11	
Brodowski	John	BA	17	15	
Brokowsk					
Brokowsky	Valentin	BA	40	614	
Bromer	Joseph	BA	22	16	
Bromer	Stanislaw	BA	17	24	
Bronatowski	Boleslaw	BA	40	6	1
Bronecky	Pawel	BA	40	614	
Bronikowsky	Tomasz	BA	40	613	
Bronseniski	Michael	BA	25	7	
Brooks	George	BA	19	4	
Broske	Andrew	BA	6	18	
Brosky	Joseph	BA	3	21	
Brosky	Joseph	BA	40	6	3
Brotsky	Ludwich	AA	18	8	
Browkowski	Anthony	BA	19	28	
Browkowski	Stanislaw	BA	40	6	3
Browonska	Valentine	BA	35	16	
Brozkowski	Leonard	BC	44	17	
Broznowicz	Joseph	BA	11	6	
Brtnikovosky	Antoni	AA	18	24	
Brucek	Mary	BA	26	18	
Bruger	Vladislow	AA	18	3	
Brujewska	Milka	BA	16	5	
Brulinski	Celestyn	BA	18	22	
Brusko	Paul	BC	48	15	
Bryanoska	Eve	BA	3	20	
Brydia	William	BA	16	5	
Brykczenski	Vincenty	BA	2	19	
Brzczynski	Joseph	BA	18	10	
Brzecko	Stanislaw	BA	2	8	
Brzesiski	Jacob	BA	15	6	
Brzezenski	Walenty	BA	19	6	
Brzozowska	Joseph	BA	8	11	
Brzozowski	Frank	BA	18	1	
Brzozowski	John	BA	17	8	
Brzozowsky	Wladislaw	BA	40	6	4
Brzynski	Paul	BA	18	4	
Buanojnoska	Eva	BA	1	24	
Buanojnoski	Peter	BA	1	16	
Bubazuk	Frank	BA	17	13	
Buc	Joseph	BA	17	33	
Buc	Teofila	BA	18	6	
Bucaczinski	Theodore	BA	5	14	
Buchucz	Peter	BA	17	36	

Last	First	CO	ED	PAG
Buchwalelski	Telfa	BA	19	33
Buck	Frank	BA	10	23
Bucykowski	William	BA	9	16
Buczek	Jan	BA	19	31
Buczkowski	Frank	BA	11	7
Buczkowski	Jacob	BA	21	14
Buczkowski	John	BA	17	16
Buczkowski	Victor	BA	11	7
Buczkowski	Wojciek	BA	19	32
Buczynski	George	BA	19	23
Budacz	Henry	BA	25	15
Budacz	Melchior	BA	18	4
Budacz	Thomas	BA	18	4
Budzanski	Frank	BA	26	11
Budziski	Michael	BA	19	18
Budzynski	Henry	BA	25	7
Bunger	John	BA	17	5
Bunk	Frank	AA	17	8b
Burbowing	William	BA	15	8
Burdel	Rosie	BA	26	4
Burkowing	Joseph	BA	15	8
Burskowski	Victor	BA	19	32
Bush	Harry	BA	19	3
Businskie	Paul	AA	17	12a
Buszak	Wojciech	BA	19	34
Buszinski	John	BA	19	30
Butchka	Joseph	BA	35	14
Butseksky	H. J.	BC	68	24
Buzinsky	Vesie	BA	22	3
Bwadka	John M.	BA	8	7
Byczynski	Maksymilian	BA	19	33
Byer	John	BA	19	35
Byerenski	Stanislaw	BA	15	4
Byoskowski	Anton	BA	18	16
Byozkoski	John	BA	9	3
Bystry	Mary	BA	17	5
Bystry	Mike	BA	26	16
Bzesynski	Theodore	BA	11	9
Caja	Karol	BA	2	9
Calawich	Michael	BA	8	7
Capalia	Joseph	BA	26	3
Carria	Joseph	BA	11	12
Cartovicski	Thomas	BA	26	9
Casavitch	Annie	AA	17	12b
Casmiercz	Michael	BA	19	11
Catkin	Anton	BA	26	7
Cebulski	Michael	BA	22	12
Cegelsky	Frank	BA	40	6 5
Cegielski	Michael	BC	48	2
Ceisla	Katherine	BA	8	9

Last	First	CO	ED	PAG
Ceslinski	Ignac	BA	9	3
Cezinski	Kostak	BA	17	25
Cgirzke	Wawrzeniec	BA	17	5
Chacka	Vladislow	AA	18	6b
Chaerlski	Joseph	BA	2	16
Chahalek	Mary	BA	2	13
Chajenski	Andrew J.	BA	19	24
Chanowsky	Frances	AA	18	16
Charlotte	Sister	BA	17	17
Chase	Michael	BA	19	1
Chazarak	Charley	BA	26	6
Checklinski	John	BA	10	16
Chelnar	Agness	AA	17	13b
Cherry	John	BA	40	6 2
Cherubine	Mary, Sister	BA	17	17
Chester	Martin	BC	68	27
Chichowak	Josef	BA	19	1
Chilinski	Ludwig	BA	18	14
Chilinsky	Victor	AA	18	6b
Chimelewski	Michael	BA	26	12
Chiniski	Jacob	BA	26	3
Chiseck	Annie	BA	4	6
Chiwatkiewicz	W.	BA	26	4
Chmelewsky	Steve	AA	18	9
Chmiel	Valentine	BA	8	5
Chmielewsky	Antony	BA	40	6 4
Chmieliski	Joseph	BA	26	7
Chmiluski	Frank	BA	19	28
Choinsky	Febs	BA	40	6 2
Chojnacka	Fodajyia	BA	8	9
Chojnacki	Franzerez	BA	19	34
Chojnowski	James	BA	19	26
Chojnowski	John	BA	25	1
Cholewerzuski	Antone	BA	15	6
Cholewinski	Joseph	BA	1	17
Chorazy	John	BA	17	16
Chraby	Stephen	BA	17	17
Chrawa	Stanslaw	BA	15	7
Chrbim	John	BA	19	31
Chrisnowski	John	BA	17	29
Christian	Felika	BA	16	1
Chrobak	Peter	BA	40	6 7
Chrobak	Wadislaw	BA	22	7
Chrowowska	Joseph	BA	2	13
Chruschmak	Harry	BA	19	6
Chrzanouski	John	BA	19	8
Chrzanowsky	Bronislawa	BA	40	612
Chrzawski	John	BA	15	10
Chswinka	Andrew	BA	8	11
Churnesko	Jozef	BA	16	12

Last	First	CO	ED	PAG
Chwinsky	Vladislow	AA	18	24
Chwinsky	Wladislow	AA	18	3
Chymny	Michael	BA	8	8
Cibisky	Alexander A.	BA	73	13
Cichocki	John	BA	2	17
Cichocki	Martin	BA	17	34
Cichon	Antonina	BA	40	6 9
Cichon	Frank	BA	5	14
Cichy	Frank	BA	16	5
Ciechanowski	Martin	BA	17	1
Cieminsky	Tomas	BA	40	614
Ciernikowsky	Joseph	BA	40	6 9
Cieslak	Joseph	BA	11	8
Cieslik	John	BA	10	11
Ciewiskie	John	AA	17	4b
Ciolba	Mary A.	BA	17	13
Cipinski	Frances	BC	45	4
Ciszechowicz	John	BA	17	6
Ciszek	George	BA	35	14
Ciutpimmeki	Peter	BC	42	11
Ciyapinska	Antoni	BA	26	10
Cochaska	William	BA	26	11
Codant	James	BA	19	24
Collins	Steven	BA	3	8
Connors	Michael	BA	19	30
Corniek	Joseph	BA	19	20
Corzyski	Michael	BA	19	11
Cosinskie	Casper	AA	17	8b
Cosiskia	Mary	AA	17	13b
Cosviska	Frank	BC	48	15
Coulaska	Joseph	BA	16	3
Cowalick	Charles	AA	14	19a
Cowdonski	John	BC	68	27
Crobubski	Charles	BA	18	15
Cryz	Anthony	BA	21	12
Curpisz	Michael	BA	18	18
Cusostki	Adam	BC	44	12
Custwicz	Kasmier	BA	18	10
Cwiek	Machiey	BA	17	31
Cywinski	William	BC	3	14
Cywinsky	Stanislaw	AA	18	13
Czajkowska	Francis	BA	3	7
Czajkowski	Joseph	BA	18	8
Czapski	Joseph	BA	11	7
Czapsky	Vicenty	BA	40	614
Czarnowsk	Ferdinand E.	BC	58	9
Czarski	John	BA	2	18
Czarski	Walenty	BA	16	2
Czekai	Jan	BA	1	18
Czerwinski	Malenty	BA	17	5

Last	First	CO	ED	PAG
Czerwinski	Peter	BA	25	6
Czeshl	John	BA	19	11
Czeswinski	Isidore	BA	17	6
Czsinski	Joseph	BA	17	16
Czwek	Martin	AA	18	13
Czyrniesvski	Franziek	BA	17	30
Czyzinski	Joseph	BA	17	5
Dabrowski	John	BA	18	15
Dabrowski	Martin	BA	11	7
Dabulski	Walter	BA	2	11
Dacewicz	Antone	BC	55	8
Damesyc	Francis	BA	17	13
Damideryk	Anton	BA	17	24
Damisyn	Michael	BA	19	14
Daniecki	Jacob	BA	8	6
Danielak	Joseph	BA	17	19
Darancz	Joseph	BA	19	7
Darlak	Joseph	BA	5	23
Das	Joseph	BA	18	4
Daugelas	Anthoney	AA	18	4a
David	Alexander	BA	1	16
Daving	Joseph	BA	1	16
Daviorinjinski	William	BA	20	13
Dczensky	Stanislaw	BA	40	6 2
Debald	Peter	BA	19	3
Debeski	George A.	BA	1	14
Debinski	Nicholas	BA	25	15
Dechruski	Richard	BA	19	35
Dedrierski	Joseph	BA	16	4
Degutes	Michael	BA	18	14
Dekowski	John	BA	19	6
DeMartin	John	BA	26	11
Demaszewicz	Michael	BA	17	13
Dembeck	Anton	BA	10	23
Dembeck	August	BA	8	9
Dembeck	August	BA	9	7
Dembeck	Frank	BA	8	4
Dembeck	John	BA	22	14
Dembeck	Valenty	BA	25	1
Dembezysky	Nellie M.	BA	40	612
Dembick	Michael	BA	8	8
Dembkowski	Pioter	BA	17	34
Dembowsky	John	AA	18	19
Dembroski	Joseph	BA	8	12
Demlenski	Katie	BA	18	18
Demluck	Walter	BA	19	23
Demoski	Boleslaus	BA	19	23
Denow	Stanislaus	BA	17	3
Dera	Stanislaus	BA	8	7
Derczyk	Stanislaus	BA	17	12

Last	First	CO	ED	PAG
Derda	Thomas	BA	16	8
Derecke	Joseph	BA	16	10
Derniewicz	Bartreni	BA	40	610
Dezensky	Stanislaw	BA	40	6 2
Deziveikovey	Casimir	BA	1	14
Dickniser	Anna	BA	25	16
Didziedzic	Kazimer	BA	17	28
Dikczykski	John	BA	35	17
DiMartin	Andrew	BA	17	8
Dimbolski	Peter	BA	24	11
Dimski	Leonard	BA	2	12
Dindiska	Mary	BA	22	17
Dinko	Ignatius	BA	25	8
Dinkovitz	Wishtor	BA	19	11
Diorush	Antoni	AA	18	16
Dirsewiecki	Wojciech	BA	16	6
Dix	Frank	BA	17	21
Dix	Frank	BA	19	10
Dix	Thomas	BA	19	8
Dlugobarski	Frank	BA	17	27
Dobelski	William	BA	1	14
Dobiecz	Joseph	BA	18	7
Dobmajcki	Nicolaus	BA	17	19
Dobrochowsky	Tomas	BA	40	6 2
Dobrowski	Yan	BA	17	35
Dobrsykowski	John	BA	40	6 1
Dobrzykaiski	Martin A.	BA	19	6
Dobrzykauski	Walenty	BA	19	31
Dobzyn	Frances	BA	18	9
Doda	Julian	BA	17	30
Doheyzoski	Wladyslaw	BA	19	5
Dolfiski	Michael	BA	19	29
Dolrowalski	Anton	BA	8	11
Dolrzykowski	James	BA	9	16
Dombkowsky	Antony	BA	40	612
Dombrowski	Joseph	BA	16	5
Dombrowsky	Antony	BA	40	6 1
Dominiak	Frank	BA	16	11
Dominik	Sabolo	BA	11	7
Domporowski	Ignatius	BA	26	19
Donaiski	Marton	BA	40	6 3
Donazski	Sophie	BA	26	14
Donoyki	Joseph	BA	1	12
Donski	Lucas	BA	2	17
Doroba	Ludwick	BA	17	22
Dorzazki	Stanislaw	BA	40	6 4
Dovby	Thomas	BA	11	5
Dowbjetzke	Martin	BC	48	7
Downs	Sophie	BA	25	4
Doyas	John L.	BA	1	17

Last	First	CO	ED	PAG
Doyemoke	John	BA	16	11
Drandower	Nogweek	BA	15	7
Drankliwez	Kate	BA	4	5
Drapezynski	Alexander	BA	3	4
Dredzinsky	Eva	BA	40	6 9
Drega	Frank	BA	18	23
Drega	Sigmund	BA	18	9
Drerubuski	Walter	BA	26	10
Dronzkiewicz	Tomas	BA	40	613
Drozd	Thomas	BA	19	27
Druga	Leopold	BA	3	20
Drush	Sima	BA	2	6
Drusth	Andrew	BA	26	7
Drustka	William	BA	26	6
Drygasz	Pawel	BA	19	10
Drzewiezki	Wladyslaw	BA	9	1
Dubeal	John	BA	11	1
Dubinski	Lasky	BA	19	5
Dubisky	Frank	BA	19	33
Duda	Michael	BA	11	10
Dudek	Joseph	BA	26	7
Dudrick	Martin	BA	19	4
Duikoisky	James	BA	14	14
Dumlick	Peter	BA	19	4
Dumphosky	John	AA	18	3
Dumpkowsky	Valentine	AA	18	16
Dumski	John	BC	68	23
Dunbowsky	Konstantin	AA	18	18
Dunson	Joseph	AA	5	5
Durmowiz	Anthony	BA	19	15
Duszewski	John	BA	1	17
Duszynski	Roman	BA	19	14
Duzack	Stan	BC	68	27
Dwiderski	John	BA	26	7
Dybies	Wladyslaw	BA	1	15
Dyinkinska	Regina	BA	18	3
Dyrgosh	Stephen	BA	17	12
Dyunnik	Frank S.	BA	15	5
Dzautek	Alex	BC	68	29
Dzcanocack	Hedwig	AA	9	1
Dzienlewska	Mary	BA	70	3
Dziewandowski	Alexander	BA	18	10
Dzinck	Anna	AA	18	20
Dzunik	Augusta	BA	9	24
Edmondski	Jacob	BA	25	7
Ehrinskowski	John	BA	17	22
Eisen	John	BA	19	30
Ekielsca	Felix A.	BA	26	4
Elert	Ignacy	BA	22	15
Elsvetak	Mary	BA	26	6

Last	First	CO	ED	PAG
Emalinska	Wladislaw	BA	40	6 4
Emelicki	Gasta	BA	19	3
Entoska	Frank	BA	19	19
Euphrosine	Mary, Sister	BA	17	17
Euska	Frank	BA	17	6
Ezdibski	Frank	BA	26	9
Fabishak	Joseph	BA	17	1
Fabishak	William	BA	17	15
Fabissak	John	BA	19	9
Fabiszak	Thomas	BA	26	8
Fabyssa	Joseph	BA	40	6 2
Faghojowska	Joseph	BA	1	15
Fakulek	Steven	BA	19	24
Falewich	Alfons	AA	18	13
Falishinick	Andrew	BA	19	3
Fasecki	Martin	BA	19	31
Fastex	Macey	BA	19	10
Feda	Theodore	BA	40	6 5
Federenko	Mike	AA	18	2
Fela	John	BA	17	5
Ference	Mary	BA	40	6 4
Ferencz	Peter	BA	17	34
Fialkowski	William	BA	35	20
Fialkowsky	Szymon	BA	40	6 9
Fibick	Woyciech	BA	17	31
Fiegiel	Wojiech W.	BA	15	13
Filgsowitz	Konstanta	BA	17	23
Filipak	George	BA	3	6
Filipkowsky	Joseph	BA	40	6 2
Fiol	Jan	BA	17	24
Fisher	August	BA	26	9
Fiskorowiz	Wladislaw	BA	17	30
Fistik	Wincenty	BA	19	10
Flawski	Mike	BA	16	4
Flojenski	Frank	BA	19	3
Fojkowski	Handrey	BA	19	16
Forenz	Frank	BA	4	1
Forsyth	Thomas	BA	3	21
Fostion	John	AA	18	6b
Fox	Nephua	BA	16	7
Fralhowski	Jacob	BA	26	2
Franchowiak	Marks	BA	8	1
Franchowitz	Anton	BC	48	16
Francis	Andrew	BA	19	28
Francizkowska	Frank	BA	25	5
Francock	Walter	BA	25	7
Frankowski	Joseph	BA	16	11
Fraser	Joseph	BC	68	29
Frawinski	Mike M.	BA	26	8
Frawiski	John	BA	15	12

Last	First	CO	ED	PAG
Frederofsky	Stanislow	AA	18	3
Fredrick	Stanley	BA	18	21
Frenchen	Frances	BA	15	13
Frieuscoski	John	BA	26	7
Fritsch	Annie	BA	18	10
Fritz	Martin J.	AA	14	19a
Fromacki	John	BA	17	33
Fryacka	Frances	BA	3	20
Fryza	Charles	BA	19	32
Fryza	Jan	BA	19	27
Fsiskey	John	BC	58	9
Gabel	Michael	BC	48	13
Gabovsky	Joseph	BC	48	10
Gackowski	John	BA	19	14
Gackowski	Tomisz	BA	5	
Gacturads	Julious	BA	1	14
Gaczar	Felicks	BA	17	1
Gaczkowski	Mike	BA	21	3
Gadek	John	BA	17	24
Gadwiga	Annie	BA	17	26
Gajdzicki	Wladislaus	BA	17	10
Gajeski	Martin	BA	19	20
Gajewski	August	BA	24	11
Gajewski	Michael	BA	22	3
Gajkowska	Bronislawa	BA	5	19
Galaczynski	Joseph	BA	17	8
Galewicz	Kazmierz	BA	40	6 6
Galuska	George	BA	14	6 3
Gamenski	Stanislaus	BA	9	5
Garilski	John	BA	11	5
Garsinski	Henry	BA	14	17
Garszynsky	Pawel	BA	40	6 2
Gasionawski	William	BA	15	13
Gaskolski	Mary	BA	8	9
Gauchman	Joseph	BA	10	14
Gavrish	Annie	AA	18	6b
Gawd	Anna	BA	5	23
Gawlik	Cazmer	BA	3	8
Gawlik	Michael	BA	5	23
Gawran	Jan	BA	2	8
Gawrys	George	BA	26	8
Gay	Michael	BA	17	31
Gaykowski	Michal	BA	16	7
Gdaski	Joseph	BA	19	2
Gease	David	BC	68	29
Geass	John	BC	68	29
Geberzt	Bronslawa	BA	35	18
Gebisky	Joseph M.	BC	49	3
Gebowski	Walter	BA	19	33
Gece	James J.	BA	17	30

16

Last	First	CO	ED	PAG
Gellesky	Dora	BA	19	4
Gelner	Andryej	BA	9	4
Geluchswski	B.	BA	14	10
Gembisky	Stanislow	AA	18	9
Genko	John	BA	26	8
Genszyns	Wojciech	BA	40	6 9
Geuse	James	BC	68	29
Gezerak	Victorie	BA	15	13
Gezeshkowiak	Harry	BA	26	12
Gibracz	Alexander	BA	19	11
Gielerski	Julian	BA	1	14
Giemski	Jan	BA	2	13
Ginchman	Michael	BA	17	26
Ginoski	William	AA	16	17a
Girynski	Michael	BA	26	2
Gitc	Annie	BA	17	32
Giwlolska	Joseph	BA	26	7
Giza	Joseph	BA	40	6 4
Gladkowski	Felix	BA	19	19
Glaucke	Wojciech	BA	19	3
Gleba	Joseph	BA	40	6 5
Glewbocky	Mateusz	BA	40	6 6
Glinka	Ignacy S.	BA	18	3
Glodek	Joseph	BA	40	611
Glodek	Stanaslonce	AA	17	4b
Glodek	Walenty	BA	26	3
Glodek	Wojciech	BA	40	611
Glombiensky	Waclaw	BA	40	610
Glowacki	Thomas	BA	19	28
Glusex	Peter	BA	19	5
Gnatowski	Antonie	BA	17	30
Godjenski	James	BA	19	18
Godnoralski	Joseph	BA	1	12
Godriski	Frank	BA	26	8
Godziewski	Joseph	BA	17	4
Godzik	Andrey	BA	19	6
Golabiecki	Joseph	AA	13	17b
Golabosbka	George M.	BA	3	6
Golaner	Anna	BA	19	2
Golanska	Stefania	BA	40	610
Golansky	Maximilian	BA	40	610
Golasynska	Rosie	BA	40	6 4
Golbuski	James	BA	19	18
Golczynski	Maryanna	BA	18	14
Goldys	John	BA	17	19
Golebienska	Jozefa	BA	1	18
Goliezewski	Felix	BA	18	16
Golinski	Henry	BA	19	19
Golobauski	Walter	BA	19	34
Golombowsky	Joseph	BA	40	610

Last	First	CO	ED	PAG
Golubski	Jacob	AA	14	19a
Golubski	Paul P.	BA	22	7
Gomboski	Peter	BC	48	9
Gomstomski	Frances	BA	15	15
Gomulka	George	BA	16	1
Goodleski	Blanche C.	BA	21	7
Gora	Wojciech	BA	19	13
Goralaski	Wladestaw	BA	26	1
Goralski	John	BA	22	11
Goralski	Lawrence	BA	19	20
Goralsky	Andreas	BA	40	6 7
Goralsky	John	BA	40	611
Gorczak	Ludwig	BA	40	614
Gorczemcz	Theodor	BA	40	6 2
Gorczewicz	Frank	BA	18	19
Gorczynsky	Joseph	BA	40	6 4
Gordack	Joseph	BC	66	15
Gordaczke	Antaiza	BA	19	20
Gorecka	George	BA	10	23
Gorezki	Wicenty	BA	1	18
Gorinski	Thomas	BA	19	9
Gorlewsky	Michael	BA	40	6 1
Gorliski	Joseph	BA	26	19
Gornowitz	Frank	BA	9	7
Gornowitz	Michael	BA	9	7
Gorny	Vincenty	BA	2	12
Gorski	Andlcek	BA	17	33
Gorski	Andy	BA	19	34
Gorski	Ludwiga	BA	17	37
Gorski	Stanislaw	BA	17	24
Gorski	Stanislaw	BA	17	33
Gorski	Walenty	BA	17	26
Gorvjleki	Stephen	BA	26	3
Gorza	Katherine	BA	19	7
Gorzenski	John	BA	1	17
Gos	Frank	BA	17	30
Goscinsky	Joseph	BA	40	6 7
Gosinskie	Vincens	AA	17	9a
Gostenia	Wladislow	AA	18	8
Gostomski	John	BA	18	17
Gostomski	Karel	BA	9	24
Gostowski	John	BA	40	6 5
Gostowski	John	BA	9	16
Goszczynski	Stanislaus	BA	21	14
Goszka	Mary	BA	25	11
Gourney	Joseph	BC	68	29
Gouskowski	Stanislau	BA	18	9
Govalsky	Marton	BA	40	6 2
Govatzski	Joseph	BA	26	3
Gozeczki	Michael	BA	24	6

Last	First	CO	ED	PAG
Gozeczki	Stephen	BA	24	6
Gozeleski	Joseph	BA	15	13
Gozeski	Ludwika	BA	17	24
Grabecki	Stanislaus	BA	9	2
Grabon	Blaze	BA	26	9
Grabowska	Mary	BA	17	3
Grabowski	Boleslaw	BA	18	10
Grabowski	John	BA	17	4
Grabowski	Valentine	BA	1	12
Grabski	John	BA	15	8
Graczavski	Phillip	BA	1	17
Graczkowski	Jacob	BA	19	15
Granka	Andrew	BA	26	19
Grat	Joseph	BA	22	11
Grauska	Alexandria	BA	26	19
Gravolski	James	BC	48	15
Grazdowski	Wetales	BA	15	14
Grcszeyniski	Piotr	BA	19	28
Grczuzk	Josephh	BA	17	13
Grebonoski	Leokadia	BA	18	13
Grecz	Madeline	BA	19	17
Greda	Kundigunda	BA	18	9
Green	Andy	AA	14	6a
Gregorek	John	AA	18	16
Greinthowski	John	BA	18	15
Grenda	Joseph	BA	25	16
Grensbrack	Machol	AA	17	14
Gresinski	Aleck	BA	26	9
Grgegonak	Teofil	BA	19	5
Gricz	Mary	BA	3	21
Gries	Johanna	BA	17	5
Grochowski	John	BA	3	10
Grocka	Theresa	BA	16	8
Grocki	Frank	BA	26	10
Gromacka	Boleslawa	BA	17	25
Grona	Dora	BA	19	13
Grondeki	Stanislaw	BA	26	8
Gronsky	Joseph	BA	40	6 8
Grosinski	Thomas	BA	17	21
Groszkowski	Felix	BA	4	2
Grotzek	Pawel	BA	17	27
Grovski	Lilly	BA	26	8
Growak	John	BA	2	20
Growski	James	BA	15	10
Gruczczynski	Vincenty	BA	17	35
Grudgzieki	John	BA	3	21
Gruno	John	BA	26	9
Grusnonski	John	BA	26	4
Grybe	Joseph	BA	18	11
Gryglik	Alexander, Sr.	BA	25	9

Last	First	CO	ED	PAG
Gryglik	Frank	BA	25	9
Gryseicka	Mary	BA	35	17
Gryzankowski	Alexandria	BA	26	16
Gryzsbski	Stephen	BA	19	24
Grzchowiax	Joseph	BA	16	6
Grzybowski	Julius	BA	8	6
Grzyma	Felix	BA	40	613
Gsbulski	Joseph	BA	1	15
Guanaski	Sophia	BA	26	8
Gulcsynski	Wawsyn	BA	2	12
Gulczewski	John	BA	18	19
Gumenznia	Peter	AA	18	9
Gurbelski	Paul	BA	16	6
Gurecki	John	BA	26	10
Gurman	Alexander	BA	3	20
Guromski	Albert	BA	16	1
Guskie	Michael	BA	26	8
Guston	George	BA	4	1
Gutewski	Jacob	BA	17	26
Gutowki	Alexander	BA	26	14
Gutowska	Kazmiera	BA	40	6 7
Gutowski	Alexander	BA	18	9
Gutowski	John	BA	17	21
Gutowski	John	BA	18	5
Gutowski	Peter	BA	18	9
Guvashki	Thomas	BA	17	25
Guyacyk	John	BA	26	14
Guyjelska	John	BA	8	14
Guzinski	Peter	BA	24	6
Gwalina	Boleslaw	BA	40	610
Gwawoski	Adolph	BA	17	19
Gyerzynski	Konstancy	BA	18	14
Gygur	Franaszek	BA	21	10
Gyvh	Eva	BA	8	11
Gzelecky	Joseph	AA	18	11
Hadzicki	John	BA	9	6
Hainlewski	Stanislaus	BA	19	13
Handushiski	Joseph	BA	19	14
Harewski	John	BA	17	22
Harkout	Michael	BA	26	10
Harley	John	BC	48	15
Harnek	John H.	BA	18	4
Harriet	Sister	BA	17	17
Harska	Stanislaus	BA	17	11
Hartka	Frank	BA	1	16
Hartman	Franciska	BA	15	15
Harzkwinski	Anton	BA	17	25
Haushard	Carl	BA	19	5
Haydak	Victor	BA	19	32
Hedwiczarski	Martin	BA	18	1

Last	First	CO	ED	PAG
Hedzel	Sebastian	BA	17	6
Hejda	Ignacy	BA	17	10
Helicinski	Peter	BA	19	25
Helinski	John	BA	17	19
Helinski	Walter	BA	18	15
Helkowzk	Alex	BA	19	20
Helowiz	Peter	BA	40	614
Hembrowski	Yan	BA	17	30
Hemoroski	Frank	BA	4	4
Hendrykowski	Frank	BA	17	5
Hennish	Henry	BA	4	4
Hensk	Stanislaw	BA	40	612
Hepner	Michael	BA	17	5
Herdgvcak	Stanislaw	BA	1	12
Herman	John	BA	40	6 2
Hetmanski	Ben	BA	17	7
Hewandowski	Albert	BA	18	6
Heyda	Theophil	BA	8	5
Hickman	Vincent J.	BA	21	3
Hiczkowski	Hadislaus	BA	18	16
Hilctowski	Valentine	BA	17	34
Hiliewicz	Stanislausa	BA	9	8
Hiliwicz	Austin	BA	15	9
Hilla	John J.	BA	26	8
Hilowoich	John	BA	26	12
Hlisczefski	Joseph	BA	17	35
Hmielewski	Adam	BA	5	23
Hodzek	Michael	BA	26	12
Hoffman	Sophia	BA	8	6
Hojnacki	Joseph	BA	6	8
Hojnoski	William	BA	19	7
Hokworski	John	BA	1	16
Holajda	Thomas	BA	8	11
Holenzyeski	Sylvester	BA	15	15
Holewinski	Stanislaw	BA	1	18
Holminiak	Vincenty	BA	22	3
Hololski	John	BA	2	18
Holopicki	John	BA	19	17
Hoorosky	Casmer	BA	26	3
Hopa	Anna	BA	40	610
Hoppa	Thomas	BA	8	12
Horagievic	Alexander	BA	4	4
Hornek	Frank	BA	18	11
Hrobocensky	Joseph	BA	19	3
Hubert	Charles	BA	18	7
Hudack	Philip	BC	48	15
Hudla	Andy	BA	26	12
Hughes	Anna	BA	15	7
Hukaszewicz	Anthony	BA	19	26
Hulley	Aloysius	BA	16	1

Last	First	CO	ED	PAG
Hurbucka	Emilia	BA	19	13
Hurzyamski	Miecylas	BA	19	8
Hybzinski	Michael	BA	18	16
Hychla	Szszepan	BA	5	3
Hyglendowski	Thomas K.	BA	2	16
Hypinor	Walenty	BA	19	4
Igar	Veronim	BA	17	35
Ignalb	John	AA	16	1b
Ignanowska	Captuder	BA	19	13
Ignatowski	Apolimary	BA	19	33
Ignatowski	Stanislaw	BA	17	28
Inata	John	BA	4	3
Irrewynski	Jan	BA	19	32
Iszkiewicz	Joseph	BA	40	6 9
Jablonski	Julia	BA	25	10
Jablonsky	John	BA	40	613
Jabloski	Jacob	BA	17	15
Jachelski	Felix	BA	26	13
Jachowski	Joseph F.	BA	9	16
Jachowski	Julian B.	BC	43	?
Jackawitz	Katarsyna	BA	17	31
Jackhelski	Joseph	BA	15	7
Jackiewicz	Jacob	BA	19	21
Jackowiak	Valentine	BA	2	7
Jackowitz	Michael	BA	22	8
Jackowski	Maryana	BA	21	10
Jackowsky	Vicenty	BA	40	610
Jacusfskie	Stonaslouce	AA	17	13a
Jaczebowski	Stanislaw	BA	19	30
Jaczycky	Valentin	BA	40	6 6
Jadworalski	Adam J.	BA	18	1
Jagoda	Andrew	BA	18	6
Jagodsinski	Jaikadeny	BA	17	7
Jagodzinski	Joseph	BA	8	8
Jagodzynsky	Michael	BA	40	6 8
Jagschinski	Jicuy	BA	19	12
Jakowski	John	BA	35	15
Jakrygowski	Jacob	AA	8	6
Jakubowski	John	BA	17	17
Jakubowski	Joseph	BA	3	7
Jaleski	Adam	BA	22	7
Jaloskie	John	AA	16	17a
James	Francis	BA	19	31
Janbick	Stefan	BA	17	27
Jancynski	Walter	BA	19	19
Janetzka	Matthais	BC	48	5
Janetzka	William	BC	48	15
Janicky	Pawel	BA	40	611
Janisinski	Maria	BA	17	26
Janka	Anton	BA	19	17

Last	First	CO	ED	PAG
Janka	John	BA	40	610
Jankewiak	James	BA	3	10
Jankiewicz	Frank	AA	16	16b
Jankiewicz	Frank	BA	14	2 2
Jankiewicz	Henry	AA	17	13b
Jankiewicz	Stanislaw	BA	73	13
Jankoski	Annie	BA	5	22
Jankowiak	Anthony	BA	8	8
Jankowiak	John	BA	26	12
Jankowski	Francis	BA	19	30
Jankowski	Jakup	BA	11	11
Jankowski	James	BA	19	4
Jankowski	John	BA	17	21
Jankowski	Joseph	BA	19	1
Jankowski	Stanislaw	BA	20	13
Jankowski	William	BA	19	4
Janoka	Wroh	BA	16	8
Janowiak	John	BA	18	8
Janowiak	Sophia	BA	19	5
Janowski	Andrew	BA	8	7
Janowski	Kostenty	BA	17	21
Janowski	Wojciech	BA	17	1
Janowsky	Antonie	BA	40	6 6
Janski	John	BA	19	32
Jantowegeska	John	BC	48	7
Janus	Anna	BA	19	13
Januskowski	John	BA	19	23
Januszuski	Annie	AA	17	11a
Januszuski	John	AA	17	11a
Janyska	Valentine	BC	7	11
Japali	Charles	BC	48	7
Japkowski	Joseph	BA	17	31
Jaran	Charles	AA	17	15
Jaras	Joseph	BA	40	6 9
Jaras	Mareu	BA	17	26
Jarockowicz	Mary	BA	17	19
Jaronczyl	Tolafila	BA	11	7
Jaroszewsky	Jacob	BA	40	6 9
Jaroszynski	John	BA	17	6
Jarowski	Ignady	BA	26	3
Jarowski	John	BA	19	2
Jarowsky	Stefan	BA	40	611
Jarshniski	Alexandr	BA	19	7
Jarsinski	Henry	BA	15	15
Jarzynski	James	BA	19	15
Jasanski	Peter	BA	18	8
Jasauska	Matthais	BA	19	13
Jasienski	Sophia	BA	18	2
Jasik	Joseph	BA	5	7
Jasinski	Teokadia	BA	5	14

Last	First	CO	ED	PAG
Jasinski	Wladislaus	BA	17	12
Jasinsky	John	BA	40	6 6
Jaskolsky	Wincent	BA	40	614
Jasomik	Wolenty	BA	8	10
Jasonowski	Charles	BA	4	1
Jassenski	Joseph	BA	35	16
Jaswmincska	Abbina	BA	17	12
Jaszynoki	Wladystaw	BA	16	10
Jaszynski	Mary	BA	18	20
Jaszynski	Mary	BA	2	349
Jawadny	Frank	BA	10	17
Jawinsky	Peter	BA	40	6 6
Jaworski	Joseph	BA	6	7
Jaworski	Michael	BA	19	10
Jaworsky	Frank	BA	1	13
Jaworsky	George	BA	1	15
Jaworsky	Henry J.	BA	1	15
Jaworsky	Ignatz	BA	1	17
Jaworsky	Leokady	BA	17	10
Jaworsky	Michael	BA	19	10
Jazdzyk	Casmer	BA	26	3
Jedmoralsky	Stanislaus	BA	9	6
Jegielski	Anton	BA	17	6
Jegierski	John	BA	40	610
Jegieski	Frank M.	BA	25	5
Jelenoski	Mary	BA	6	8
Jelinski	Martin	BA	5	7
Jendrashewitz	William J.	BA	18	20
Jendrejerska	Mary	BA	19	31
Jendrek	Frank	BA	46	5
Jentryewski	Helen	BA	14	14
Jeshovisk	Versuske	AA	17	9b
Jeukuberuk	Stanislaw	BA	16	2
Jilski	Segorirm	BA	17	25
Jiruski	William	BA	19	4
Jmala	Walenty	BA	1	17
Johnas	Annie	BA	26	7
Johusky	Stanislau	BC	51	11
Jomkiewia	Joseph	BA	15	12
Jones	Louis J.	BA	9	5
Joran	Martin	BA	22	11
Joshulska	Michael	BA	26	12
Jozchuski	Brnfrez	BA	19	7
Jozefa	Marek	BA	35	18
Jsansinzki	Martin	BA	26	9
Jsksas	Julius	BA	26	3
Jubal	Martin	BC	53	11
Jubick	Agness	AA	17	12b
Jubkouski	Mike	BA	19	31
Jugelewicz	Frank	BA	22	3

24

Last	First	CO	ED	PAG
Jugierski	Michael	BA	19	8
Julia	Sister	BA	17	17
Jurak	Henry	BA	40	6 6
Juris	John	BA	40	6 8
Juris	Kazmierz	BA	40	6 4
Juris	Martin	BA	40	6 8
Juszczewski	Raymond	BA	14	1 7
Jutowski	Boleslaw	BA	1	15
Juwkowski	Jacob	BA	17	6
Jzebowski	John	BA	1	18
Jzikowski	Edward	BA	17	25
Kabrensky	Antony	BA	40	6 5
Kacholozki	Martin	BA	26	11
Kacsinski	Joseph	BA	26	9
Kaczmarek	Mary	BA	40	6 8
Kaczorowski	John	BC	68	24
Kaczynski	Jacob	BA	35	14
Kadlubowski	Ignatya	BA	35	20
Kadzimierack	Joseph	AA	18	16
Kaenecke	John	BA	19	22
Kaezorowska	Joseph	BC	48	12
Kafel	John	BA	40	613
Kafska	Sylvester	BA	26	5
Kahler	Katie	BA	19	10
Kaight	Tena	BC	48	9
Kainmuska	John	BA	16	8
Kaiser	Thomas	BC	66	15
Kaiske	Frances	BA	40	610
Kajduk	Mary	BA	8	9
Kakowski	Sadie	BA	17	4
Kalendik	Felix	BA	19	16
Kalinowski	Joseph	BA	21	4
Kalinowski	Stanislaw	BA	2	10
Kalinowsky	Alexander	BA	40	6 2
Kalinowsky	Stephen	BA	40	6 8
Kalinsak	George	BA	8	5
Kalinski	John	BA	24	6
Kalkowski	Victor	BA	14	11
Kalnak	John	AA	17	9a
Kalscypiski	Anthony	BA	19	22
Kalsczynski	Tom	BA	19	22
Kalska	Maria	BA	40	614
Kalwa	Bronislaw	BA	21	3
Kamda	Anton	BA	17	12
Kamiansky	Wladislow	AA	18	9
Kamienski	John	BA	5	13
Kaminski	Piotr	BA	17	4
Kaminsky	Henry	BA	19	29
Kaminsky	Leon	BA	40	612
Kamisky	Stanislaw	BA	40	6 7

Last	First	CO	ED	PAG
Kamyowski	John	BA	11	3
Kamzeski	John	BA	19	33
Kandy	Joseph	BA	17	5
Kanechiak	Mary	BA	19	18
Kanecki	Wawzynk	BA	17	32
Kaneczky	Walenty	BA	17	32
Kanieck	Konstenty	BA	19	14
Kaniecki	Frank	BA	1	17
Kanlinski	Jacob	BA	11	4
Kannesky	Wadyslaw	BA	35	14
Kansinska	Rosalie	BA	17	25
Kantorski	John	BA	18	19
Kanva	Vincent	BA	3	22
Kapa	Joseph	BA	26	14
Kapisjak	John	BA	19	29
Kapriryk	Thomas	BA	17	5
Kaprisorenski	Michael	BA	1	16
Karaban	Anton	BA	18	14
Karaczewski	Frank	BA	17	13
Karas	Sophia	BA	19	17
Karcnewska	Anton	BA	8	9
Karcz	Franciszek	BA	17	25
Karczski	Leon	BA	8	9
Kardas	John	BA	40	6 7
Kardecka	Josephine	BA	17	25
Kares	Andrew	BA	5	12
Karezeswski	Joseph	BA	15	13
Karichnewski	Martin	BA	17	30
Karkowska	Katerzyna	BA	40	613
Karls	Adam	BA	26	9
Karnlis	Gerhaza	BA	17	32
Karnoska	Franciska	BA	17	25
Karolski	Frank	BA	25	1
Karoz	Kazmiess	BA	3	10
Karpansak	Alexander	BA	26	19
Karpinski	Alexander	BA	26	3
Karpinski	John L.	BA	18	16
Karpinsky	Frank	AA	18	3
Karpomez	Peter	BA	2	17
Karsick	Jacob	BA	2	7
Karta	Anna	BA	19	11
Karvorski	Joseph, Sr.	BA	17	28
Karwacka	Michael	BA	2	11
Karwacka	Walynty	BA	2	11
Karwacki	John F.	BA	2	7
Kasewitz	Frank	BA	17	25
Kasfby	Albert	BA	15	7
Kashak	Joseph	BA	19	11
Kasimierski	Nicolas	BA	17	16
Kasinski	Stanaslaus	BA	19	10

Last	First	CO	ED	PAG
Kaspar	Sophia	BA	26	19
Kasper	Martin	BA	4	4
Kasprowicz	Frank	BA	25	9
Kastask	Peter	BA	1	13
Kaszubinsky	Frank	AA	18	16
Kaszubinsky	John	AA	18	16
Kaszubski	Marian	BA	26	16
Kaszuzak	James	BA	19	11
Katecei	Ignacy	BA	19	3
Katowicz	Charles R.	BA	17	13
Katzinski	Adam	BA	17	24
Kaupinski	Alexander	BC	66	15
Kautuska	James	BA	26	11
Kavalefsky	Steve J.	AA	18	3
Kavernyski	Andrew	BA	1	17
Kawa	Tekla	BA	18	19
Kawacjki	Walenty	BA	18	8
Kawalefsky	John	AA	18	20
Kawecki	Jacob	BA	8	8
Kawelusky	Warren	AA	17	11a
Kawicki	Walter	BA	18	21
Kazemarck	John	BA	3	7
Kazmierczak	Joseph	BA	14	6
Kedezejewski	William	BC	66	15
Kedring	John	BA	3	69
Kedring	Stanistaw	BA	26	19
Kedziererski	Josef	BA	19	15
Kelan	Wojciech	BA	19	12
Kelly	Anna	BA	40	6 4
Kelminiak	Joseph J.	BA	8	8
Kelner	Constanty	BA	1	14
Kempka	Pawel	BA	17	7
Kender	William	BC	68	28
Kendzierski	Adam J.	BA	3	6
Kendziersky	Martin	BA	40	612
Kendzieski	Michael	BA	19	34
Kennick	Edward	BA	18	22
Kenny	Michael	BA	1	17
Kensicki	Joseph	BC	48	23
Kentrzgewski	Robert	BA	9	6
Kepec	Wojcisch	BA	17	5
Kereal	Andrew	BA	3	8
Kevsinski	Adam	BA	1	16
KeyJare	Joseph T.	BA	19	31
Kezejewska	Mary	BA	9	2
Kezmier	Michael	BA	40	6 7
Kibuski	Thomas	BA	22	16
Kic	Peter	BA	8	5
Kicialewski	Czaclav	BA	3	19
Kicialewski	Joseph	BA	35	19

Last	First	CO	ED	PAG
Kidesejeski	Frank	BA	8	4
Kieczal	Jacob	BA	17	10
Kiel	Mary	BA	9	24
Kierpko	Wojdacek	BA	35	11
Kiewogloski	James	BA	21	3
Kilcey	Gus	BA	19	25
Kilenski	Adam	BA	17	25
Kilkowski	Frank	BA	22	17
Kilkowski	Martin	BA	21	3
Kilkowsky	Maryan	BA	40	6 4
Kintinsky	Frank	BA	17	25
Kiper	Thomas	BA	19	24
Kirdonski	Michael	BA	5	17
Kisielewsky	Seraryn	BA	35	20
Kisner	Joseph	BA	16	8
Kiwoliwysk	Stanaslaw	BA	4	3
Kizowski	John	BA	17	22
Klein	George	BC	55	8
Klesczefski	Ludwig	BA	17	37
Klesczynski	George	BA	25	15
Kleszcynska	Catherine	BA	11	7
Klimck	Paul	BA	8	5
Klimeck	Victor	BA	17	19
Klinek	Adam	BA	17	7
Klinouski	Henry	BA	19	11
Klinowski	Frank	BA	17	27
Klionofski	Joseph	BA	18	19
Kloc	Michel	BA	16	5
Klokoski	Andrew	BA	3	22
Klonowski	Adam	BA	21	7
Klonowski	Joseph	BA	16	5
Klos	Stanislaus	BA	17	19
Klosinska	Walenty	BA	2	13
Kluchinski	John	BA	1	17
Klucznik	Hilno	BA	17	10
Kluczyk	Constance	BA	19	20
Klusicki	Michael	BA	19	5
Klymonuski	Michael	BA	19	25
Klyski	Henry	BA	17	13
Klyusziuth	Wilhelm	BA	19	30
Klywszundt	John	BA	19	13
Klywszundt	Michael	BA	19	13
Kmieriak	George	BA	15	7
Knabe	Joseph	BA	17	3
Knafik	Stanislaus	BA	11	7
Knasiak	Jacob	BA	22	11
Kneawse	Mary	BA	40	6 8
Kninski	Alexander	BA	17	27
Knjsiak	Joseph	BA	26	6
Knovena	Joseph	BA	18	9

Last	First	CO	ED	PAG
Knvck	Egnats	AA	17	11
Knzknda	Conrad	BA	17	37
Kobat	Radsa	BA	15	15
Kobetch	Frank	AA	18	4
Kobylinski	Karol	BA	17	7
Kobylski	Julian	BA	15	5
Kobzan	Juljan	BA	17	10
Kocawa	Jan	BA	10	16
Kocent	Andrew	BA	5	14
Kocent	Anton	BA	8	8
Kocgrosky	Michael	BA	19	4
Koch	Harry W.	BA	3	7
Kochanowski	Joseph	BA	17	1
Kochanski	Franciska	BA	17	13
Kochanski	George	BA	19	1
Kochanski	Stanislaus	BA	17	16
Kochlszewski	Jadsz	BA	14	1 7
Kocienski	John	BA	19	30
Kocyan	John A.	BA	10	7
Kocyke	Joseph	BA	26	10
Koczenski	Stanislaw	BA	17	28
Koczorowsky	Mary	BA	40	6 9
Kofikoski	Smitle	BA	2	18
Kofskey	Michael	BC	68	24
Kofsky	George	BC	68	29
Kogat	Frank	BA	19	34
Kogowski	Waditas	BA	1	89
Kohwazk	Annie	BA	26	14
Koinovick	Frank	BA	16	4
Kolachowski	Audney	BA	17	19
Kolacz	Thomas	BA	18	2
Kolakavitch	Frank	AA	17	15
Kolakowski	Joseph	BA	19	5
Kolakowski	Joseph	BA	35	20
Kolb	John	BA	2	17
Kolinewa	Mary	BA	26	3
Kolinski	George	BA	26	11
Kolisiskie	Frank	AA	17	13b
Kolkowski	Joseph	BA	8	3
Kollarz	Charles, Rev.	AA	17	15
Kolleanwicki	Katherine	BA	19	35
Kolodsyski	Michael	BA	19	23
Kolokosski	Joseph	BA	19	17
Kolovinski	Mary	BA	2	13
Kolozy	John	BA	1	15
Kolski	Alexander	BA	15	11
Kolub	Alexander	BA	2	17
Kolup	James	BC	66	15
Kolvaleski	John	BA	25	10
Kolwilski	James	BA	14	17

Last	First	CO	ED	PAG
Komelsky	John	BA	40	6 8
Konarzofski	Frank	BA	1	13
Koneszna	John	BA	1	13
Konielski	Joseph	BA	26	11
Konofska	Joseph	BA	2	17
Konofska	Teopl	BA	2	17
Konopacka	Blazej	BA	8	14
Kontzsky	George	BA	26	6
Kopcszinski	Lizzie	BA	4	5
Kopera	Joseph	BA	22	16
Kopera	Kazmer	BA	17	28
Kopieczyk	Joseph	BA	40	613
Kopinska	Josephine	BA	17	16
Kopinski	Frank	BC	44	17
Kopitch	Joseph	AA	18	6b
Koplanczk	Joseph	BA	4	5
Koprowski	Joseph	BA	2	13
Kopycinski	Theodore	BA	9	13
Kordas	Joseph	BA	19	12
Kordonski	Josef	BA	2	13
Kordonski	Joseph	BA	3	8
Kordonski	Walenty	BA	2	18
Kordovski	Wawszyn	BA	2	13
Koretkowsky	Vladislow	AA	18	11
Korlowska	James	BA	9	6
Kororowski	Michael	BA	17	33
Koroveski	Joseph	BC	48	10
Korowkowski	Stanislaw	BA	26	7
Korprowski	Frank	BA	1	14
Koryasyewski	Frank	BA	86	8
Korycki	John	BA	18	23
Korytowski	Christian	BA	6	1
Korzinska	Pelgra	BA	19	12
Korzynowsky	Cerin	BA	40	6 9
Kosajchski	Francia	BA	19	9
Kosakowski	Joseph	BA	26	4
Kosakowsky	Leon	BA	40	611
Kosalowsky	Naopol	BA	40	6 7
Koscinsky	Wincenty	BA	40	6 1
Koserski	Julius	BA	19	3
Koshiskie	Joseph	AA	17	15
Kosiba	Wojcich	BA	5	22
Kosinski	Felix	BA	2	17
Kosinskie	August	AA	17	13a
Koslofskie	Joseph	AA	17	14a
Koslovski	August	BA	19	25
Kostoski	James	BA	18	8
Kostowski	John	BA	17	19
Kosycki	Stephen	BA	24	3
Kosyki	Adam	BA	19	25

Last	First	CO	ED	PAG
Kot	Mary	BA	26	7
Kotowschski	Alex	BA	19	5
Kotowsky	Boleslaw	BA	40	6 4
Kotsdrachtski	Boroly	BA	26	13
Kouski	James	BA	26	14
Kovalewski	Stansilaus	BA	19	8
Kovalske	Mike	BA	21	3
Kovieczny	Wojciech	BA	17	12
Kovjack	Henry	BC	48	15
Kowalauski	Martin	BA	19	31
Kowaleski	Joseph H.	BA	17	33
Kowalewski	Andrew	BA	4	3
Kowalewski	Jacob	BA	17	12
Kowalewski	John W.	BA	19	24
Kowalewski	Martin	BA	18	9
Kowalewski	Stanislau	BA	19	9
Kowaloska	Kamila	BA	17	18
Kowalowski	Stanislaus	BA	17	29
Kowalska	Frank	BA	5	22
Kowalski	Anna	BA	19	13
Kowalski	Anton	BA	18	8
Kowalski	Elizabeth	BA	16	11
Kowalski	Frank	BA	18	9
Kowalski	Frank	BA	3	22
Kowalski	Frank B.	BA	6	18
Kowalski	Jacob	BA	26	19
Kowalski	John	BA	2	13
Kowalski	John	BA	25	10
Kowalski	Joseph	BA	18	6
Kowalski	Rose P.	BA	19	31
Kowalski	Stanislaus	BC	48	5
Kowalski	Stanislaw	BA	17	26
Kowalski	Stanislaw	BA	18	6
Kowalski	Stephen	BA	21	7
Kowalski	Stevan	BA	21	4
Kowalsky	Antony	BA	40	610
Kowartkska	John	BA	9	26
Kowinski	George	BA	11	9
Kowlowski	John	BA	11	7
Kowlsfki	Peter	BC	48	7
Kozak	Joseph	BA	40	6 4
Kozepka	Peter	BA	26	19
Kozepsky	Kazimer	AA	18	16
Kozera	Alexander	BA	19	23
Kozews	Walter	BC	68	24
Kozierski	Stanislaw	BA	19	34
Kozlawski	Adam	BA	11	1
Kozloska	Joseph	BA	26	1
Kozlowski	John	BA	25	8
Kozlowski	John	BA	26	19

Last	First	CO	ED	PAG
Kozlowski	John	BA	40	6 7
Kozlowski	Joseph	BA	25	7
Kozlowski	Joseph	BA	8	4
Kozlowski	Stanislaus	BA	15	2
Kozlowsky	Antony	BA	40	614
Kozlowsky	Michael	BA	40	6 4
Kozlowsky	Tomas	BA	40	614
Kozlsoski	Joseph	BA	17	22
Kozniersky	Michael	BA	40	6 6
Kozowski	James	BA	1	16
Koztowski	Anthony	BA	26	7
Kraiger	Tina	BA	17	24
Kralik	Tomacz	BA	40	610
Kramer	Jadwiga J.	BA	8	8
Krans	Paul	BA	17	23
Kraslia	John	BA	18	16
Kratz	Charles	BA	17	4
Kraus	Lillian	BA	9	26
Krauska	Agnes	BA	26	11
Krawczynski	George	BA	19	17
Krawzyk	Anthony	BA	15	10
Kraz	Martin	BA	17	30
Krazinski	Walenty	BA	1	16
Krefka	Anthony	BA	19	33
Krelinski	Mary	BC	48	14
Kremski	Joseph	BA	9	8
Kric	John	BA	17	5
Krieger	John E.	BA	4	1
Kriniciak	John	BA	9	8
Kriniciak	Joseph	BA	9	8
Krishofka	Katharine	BA	22	16
Kristineck	Wladislaw	BA	40	6 9
Kristkievicz	Stanislaw	BA	40	612
Krjiskowski	Michael	BA	19	33
Krmarra	Frank	BA	19	23
Krol	James	BA	19	7
Krol	John	BA	19	5
Krol	Katherina	BA	18	4
Krolcarek	Marcin	BA	16	3
Krolezyk	Peter	BA	16	3
Kromak	Joseph	BA	21	11
Kropp	Felix	BA	16	4
Kropp	Frank	BA	16	9
Kroskowski	Frank	BA	17	26
Krouchuski	Jacob	BA	18	15
Krouchuski	William	BA	18	15
Krowkowski	Carl	BA	4	1
Krowszyk	Stanislaus	BA	19	12
Krue	Joseph	BA	25	5
Kruger	James	BA	19	20

Last	First	CO	ED	PAG
Kruger	Roman	BA	19	23
Krugiski	Martin	BA	19	33
Kruk	John	BA	40	6 4
Krulikowski	Josef	BA	2	8
Krupensick	Michael	BA	17	19
Krusheck	Stanislow	AA	18	13
Krusinski	Casimar	BA	15	10
Krusniewski	Benjamin	BA	5	14
Kruzla	Peter	BA	5	17
Krygier	Joseph	BA	19	12
Krymski	Pawel	BA	11	6
Krymski	Stanislaus	BA	9	16
Krysiak	Stephan	BA	19	13
Kryvoch	Julia	BA	16	7
Ksiazck	Anna	BA	8	11
Ksiczogsolska	John	BA	21	3
Ksiniski	Andy	BA	19	19
Kuava	Wadwaf	BA	18	6
Kubisky	Felix	BA	40	6 3
Kubrvik	Mary	BA	15	9
Kuc	Henry	BA	17	22
Kuc	John	BA	26	18
Kuc	John	BA	40	6 4
Kuc	Joseph	BA	35	15
Kuc	Michael	BA	9	3
Kuc	Samuel	BA	40	613
Kuc	Stephen	BA	17	22
Kuchanski	Welenty	BA	17	5
Kucharski	John	BA	17	10
Kuchta	Anton	BA	8	10
Kuchta	John	BA	8	10
Kuczarski	John	BA	17	8
Kuczewski	Joseph	BA	22	16
Kuczewski	Kasmier	BA	18	5
Kuczewsky	Stanislaw	BA	40	612
Kuczynski	Antony	BA	18	6
Kuczynski	Constant	BA	17	10
Kuczynski	Paul	BA	19	6
Kudak	Peter	BA	26	4
Kudges	Janus	BA	15	9
Kudlok	Frank	BA	19	25
Kughta	Stefan	BA	18	7
Kugowski	Waditas	BA	3	10
Kuinowsky	Wladislow	AA	18	16
Kujawa	Antone	BA	2	8
Kujtineak	Wojciech	BA	8	8
Kulack	Joseph	BA	9	4
Kulacki	Ludwik	BA	21	10
Kulacky	Lukasz	BA	40	6 2
Kulcinski	John	BA	18	13

Last	First	CO	ED	PAG
Kulecs	Frank	BA	4	4
Kulesa	John	BA	40	6 1
Kulicinic	Anton	BC	42	1
Kuliczwicz	Antonie	BA	11	7
Kulinski	Michael	BA	19	18
Kulinski	Walter	BA	17	19
Kuliszewski	Edward	BA	19	13
Kulski	Antonie W.	BA	17	29
Kulsonski	Anton	BA	3	7
Kumner	Jonsica	BA	15	11
Kupeczki	Wallace	BA	17	30
Kurak	Thomas	BA	26	9
Kurcab	Antoni	BA	5	24
Kurek	Agnes	BA	8	5
Kurek	Franciska	BA	8	11
Kurek	John	BA	16	8
Kurowski	Frank	BA	14	11
Kurowski	Jacob	BA	17	24
Kurowski	Joseph J.	BA	3	8
Kurowski	Michael	BA	17	35
Kurowsky	Joseph	BC	48	14
Kus	Joseph	BA	17	25
Kutz	Frank	BA	35	16
Kutz	Joseph	BA	18	9
Kutz	Stanislaus	AA	12	7
Kuyawa	Albert G.	BA	1	13
Kuyawa	Francis	BA	9	1
Kuyawa	Magdeline	AA	5	5
Kuzinski	Lears	BA	14	2
Kuzma	Michael	BA	8	5
Kuzmarski	Joseph	BA	17	13
Kuzyski	Stanislaw	BA	26	4
Kuzzlau	John	BA	26	6
Kwaksnik	John	BA	18	14
Kwasink	Stephen	BA	2	99
Kwasnieski	Andy	BA	26	15
Kwasnink	Joseph	BA	17	8
Kwercinski	Wladyslaw	BA	14	1 7
Kwiakouski	Casimi	BA	4	2
Kwiatkowska	Valeria	BA	17	8
Kwiatkowski	Andrew	BA	19	14
Kwiatkowski	John	BA	17	4
Kwiatkowski	Lizzie	BA	17	27
Kwiatkowski	Martin	BA	17	22
Kwiatkowski	Michael	BA	40	6 9
Kwiatkowski	Vincent	BA	8	11
Kwiatkowsky	Henryk	BA	40	6 5
Kwiocki	Ignatius	BA	17	12
Kwizkowski	Joseph	BA	1	14
Kworta	Agata	BA	17	31

Last	First	CO	ED	PAG
Labougiski	Ignatius	BA	26	14
Ladna	Ignatius	BA	17	21
Lagunski	John	BA	26	13
Lakowski	Constantine	BA	22	14
Lakuis	Faderesz	BA	19	35
Lalicki	Michael	BA	8	14
Lamenski	James L.	BA	10	22
Lamenski	Michael	BA	8	6
Laminski	Frank	BA	2	8
Lamparske	John	BC	45	4
Lancovski	Theresa	BA	8	11
Lang	Agnes	BA	3	2
Langoski	John	BA	19	20
Lansanski	John	BA	19	5
Lasinsky	Dominik	AA	18	4a
Laskowski	Antony	BA	17	16
Lathanski	M.	BA	16	4
Lauchinski	Andy	BA	19	5
Lavicka	Michel	BA	14	2
Lawence	Minnie	BA	2	18
Lawinsky	Vincent	BA	17	8
Lawrence	Frank	BA	5	23
Lawska	John	BA	17	7
Lazarwiz	Rosa	BA	14	17
Lazeski	Felix	BA	17	19
Lazorek	Wojcheck	BA	5	23
Lechert	Joseph F.	BA	9	6
Lechowich	Joseph	AA	18	3
Lefkiewicz	Dominic	BC	48	15
Legestawa	Tina	BA	19	11
Lehchek	Alexander	BA	26	18
Leiwilski	Josephine	BA	19	7
Lenart	Maria	BA	19	13
Lendz	Joseph	BA	19	1
Lentz	John	BA	19	33
Lentz	Martin	BA	18	13
Lepszuwna	Olszula	BA	40	612
Lerwck	Wladislawa	AA	18	18
Leschinsky	Hermana	BA	88	18
Leshowa	Julian S.	BA	18	5
Lesiak	Franciszek	BA	5	23
Lesiecki	Jacob	BA	15	7
Lesinewski	Antonie	BA	17	28
Leski	Mary	BA	18	16
Lessey	George	BA	19	20
Levandovski	Walter	BA	14	1 7
Levanduski	Joseph	BA	26	5
Levinsky	John	AA	18	16
Levonduski	James	BA	26	11
Lewandowski	Andrew	BA	18	9

Last	First	CO	ED	PAG
Lewandowski	Andy	BA	19	8
Lewandowski	Ignatius	BA	16	12
Lewandowski	John	BA	16	11
Lewandowski	Josef	BA	19	13
Lewandowski	Josef	BA	19	26
Lewandowski	Joseph	BA	1	16
Lewandowski	Maryanna	BA	17	35
Lewandowski	Michel	BA	17	24
Lewandowski	Stephen	BA	35	20
Lewandowski	Sygmont	BA	17	24
Lewandowski	Thomas	BA	24	1
Lewandowski	Waleryan	BA	17	5
Lewandowsky	Frank	BA	40	6 5
Lewandowsky	Kazimer	AA	18	9
Lewandowsky	Leopold	BA	40	6 3
Lewenwowski	Frank	BA	17	32
Lewinski	Joseph	BA	18	13
Lewinsky	James	BA	25	16
Leyrak	Joseph	BA	17	19
Libinski	James	BC	44	24
Lickert	William	BA	3	21
Lignowska	Anna	BA	19	6
Lihinoffyz	Rosalia	BA	3	6
Lijewski	John	BA	25	7
Likorski	Peter	BA	25	9
Limonoch	Wojciech	BA	17	33
Linety	Wladislaus	BA	17	6
Linskeys	Eva	BC	55	18
Lipinski	Albert	BA	19	8
Lipinski	Josephine	BA	17	1
Lipinski	Madislaw	BA	10	21
Lipka	Adalbert	BA	17	35
Lipka	Martin	BA	14	10
Lipka	Woricek	BA	22	11
Lipski	John	BA	9	6
Lipsky	Helena	AA	18	2
Lischinsky	Alexander	AA	18	18
Lisek	Bartholomew	BA	8	6
Lisicki	Joseph	BA	26	3
Lisiecki	Ignacy	BA	3	9
Lisiezki	Ludwig	BA	17	33
Literski	Adam F.	BA	21	10
Literski	Anton	BA	19	7
Litinski	Mary	BA	21	10
Litwonska	John J.	BA	17	35
Loberetyesin	Lasser	BA	19	5
Loch	George	BC	48	16
Lock	Frank	BC	68	29
Lodecka	Ernie	BA	17	34
Loek	Yan	BA	17	30

36

Last	First	CO	ED	PAG		
Lohinski	William	BA	19	4		
Lohn	Louisa	BA	18	1		
Lohodziski	Stanislau	BA	19	15		
Lomisky	John	BA	40	614		
Lonek	Agnes	BA	19	25		
Lonex	Thomas	BA	19	4		
Lopinski	William	AA	19	4		
Lorek	Frank	BA	19	1		
Lorek	Michalina	BA	16	8		
Loreke	Maryanna	BA	15	7		
Lotkouski	Michael	BA	19	15		
Lovine	George	BA	17	5		
Lozanski	Wladyslaw	BA	18	6		
Lubava	Anna	BA	15	7		
Lubbish	Henry	BA	14	1	7	
Lubinski	Barbara C.	BA	60	8		
Lubinsky	Stanislaw	BA	40	6	5	
Luckowska	Joseph	BC	49	3		
Luczensky	Stanislaw	BA	40	6	7	
Luczkowski	James	BC	49	13		
Luja	Joseph	BA	5	19		
Lukaszewiks	Frank	BA	3	8		
Lukaszoraski	John	BA	16	5		
Lukesazny	Joseph	BA	19	12		
Lukowski	Biguneto	BA	19	22		
Lushefski	Peter	BA	19	28		
Luskischuski	Viech	BA	19	11		
Luskowski	Henry	BA	17	28		
Luysmunski	August	BA	19	15		
Lvosdof	Lawrence	BA	22	17		
Lyaodocka	Mary	BA	35	18		
Lyardocka	Yojcek	BA	35	18		
Lylewski	George	BA	17	30		
Lysniewski	Jan	BA	26	5		
Lythacski	Ida	BA	16	1		
Lzybroski	Joseph G.	BA	18	16		
Lzydlauski	Boseslaus	BA	19	20		
Macek	Frances	BA	26	2		
Macek	Miela	BA	40	6	5	
Mach	Frank	BA	40	6	6	
Mach	Marian	BA	19	6		
Macha	Joseph	BA	17	6		
Machalak	Lucy	BA	17	33		
Macher	Peter	BA	17	37		
Machjeski	Marian	BC	68	29		
Machku	Andrew	BA	19	10		
Machnaik	Antonie	BA	17	27		
Machsynski	Alex	BA	19	10		
Maciewjewski	Henry J.	BA	18	8		
Mackowiak	Mary	BA	10	7		

Last	First.	CO	ED	PAG
Mackowiak	Stefan	BA	8	7
Macly	Waclau	BA	18	7
Macrznak	Lawrence	BA	19	10
Maculski	Charles	BC	48	10
Maczeinniec	Konstanti	BA	17	27
Maczewitz	Michael	BA	17	34
Maczka	Walenty	BA	17	34
Maday	John	BA	40	614
Madra	Polin E.	BA	3	6
Madyski	Joseph	BA	19	18
Maenzysski	Peter	BA	19	10
Mafebanski	George	BA	1	14
Magerowic	Dora	BA	22	11
Mahalski	Alex	BC	68	28
Mahasky	Joseph	BC	68	29
Maichkavitz	Joseph	BA	19	11
Majcharz	Kazimer	BA	15	2
Majchrak	John	BA	17	13
Majeheyki	Joe	BA	19	32
Majewsky	Alexander	BA	40	611
Majka	Ignac	BA	40	6 9
Majka	Jacenty	BA	8	14
Majka	John	BA	17	3
Majka	Peter	BA	26	5
Makaski	John	BA	1	17
Makowiecki	Wincent	BA	40	614
Makowski	Annie	BA	15	7
Makowski	John	BA	17	24
Makowski	John	BA	9	13
Makraska	Maryanna	BA	40	6 5
Makrina	Mary, Sister	BA	17	17
Malachowsky	Frank	BA	40	614
Malacki	Joseph	BA	18	12
Malanowski	Joseph	BA	3	21
Malders	William F.	BA	4	1
Malecki	Michel	BA	16	3
Maleska	Piolo	BA	8	11
Maleski	Martin	BC	48	9
Maletzka	Frank	BA	17	21
Malezski	Walter	BA	16	5
Malicke	James	BA	10	14
Malicki	Valenty	BA	40	610
Malikowsky	John	BA	40	6 4
Malinoski	Joseph	BA	1	17
Malinowski	Adam	BA	17	25
Malinowski	Antonie	BA	21	12
Malinowski	Julian	BA	6	3
Malinowski	Kazimer	BA	17	25
Malinowski	Michall	BA	19	4
Malinowski	Peter	BA	24	1

38

Last	First	CO	ED	PAG
Malinowski	Stanislaw	BA	17	33
Malinowski	Wincenty	BA	17	34
Malinowsky	Alexander	AA	18	14
Malinski	John	BA	25	8
Maliserki	Francis	BA	15	12
Malsewski	Lippert	BA	17	25
Malvitch	Zofia	BA	21	4
Malyshiski	Casimir	BA	17	16
Mam	Peter	BA	18	13
Maniewski	Peter	BA	17	5
Manksiswitz	Marting	BA	15	7
Manski	Joseph	BC	48	15
Mantik	Frank	BA	19	29
Mantik	William	BC	45	4
Mapieralski	Lucy	BA	8	9
Marchinski	John	BA	18	9
Marchlewicz	John	BA	18	8
Marcinki	Paul	BA	19	14
Marcinkow	Anna	BA	17	30
Marcinkowski	Stefan	BA	19	26
Marcoski	Eva	BA	1	16
Marecka	Theofila	BA	17	29
Marecki	Stanislaum	BA	2	18
Marek	Jan	BA	35	18
Mareski	Wilko	BA	16	9
Margunek	Marcelia	BA	1	13
Marines	Mary	BA	19	29
Marjewski	Frank	BA	25	8
Markiewicz	John	BA	18	10
Markiewicz	John	BA	2	18
Markiewicz	Michael	BA	22	15
Markiewis	Wojcieth	BA	5	16
Markow	Kzimer	BA	16	25
Marlzciana	Adam	BA	25	10
Marmasz	Alexander	BA	5	17
Marsh	John	BA	26	10
Marshall	Michael	BA	5	13
Marski	Antone J.	BA	3	4
Marski	John T.	BA	15	15
Marski	Joseph	BA	3	2
Marski	Joseph A.	BA	60	8
Marski	Justina	BA	60	8
Marski	Michael	BA	8	14
Marskotka	Peter	BA	26	6
Martauski	Frank	BA	19	20
Martskin	Bronislow	AA	17	11a
Maruv	John	BA	8	8
Marzceki	Francis	BA	19	4
Marzulis	Joseph	BA	17	24
Mashinska	Frances	BA	21	14

Last	First	CO	ED	PAG	
Maskill	Teodor	BA	19	1	
Maskll	Joseph	BA	19	1	
Maslowski	Wojciech	BA	19	10	
Masowa	Alexander	BA	17	19	
Matanoski	Anton	AA	8	2	
Matassek	Julian	BA	26	5	
Matecki	John	BC	48	9	
Matek	Frank	BA	19	10	
Materacki	Joseph	BA	35	20	
Mateuszek	Felex	AA	18	9	
Matitskie	Frank	AA	17	8b	
Matouschuk	Thomas	AA	17	11b	
Matushefsky	Frank	AA	18	7	
Matusky	Ernerick	AA	14	19a	
Matussewski	James	BA	8	6	
Matuszek	Jan	BA	1	13	
May	Joseph	BA	17	37	
Mayeliski	Walenty	BA	19	10	
Mayewsky	Antoni	AA	18	24	
Mazec	Rose	BA	17	6	
Mazefski	Jacob	BA	17	23	
Mazgowski	James	BA	1	17	
Mazon	Annie	BA	18	22	
Mazon	Blzy	BA	18	10	
Mazor	Michael	BA	40	6	4
Mazur	Adelbert	BA	19	12	
Mazurowski	Walentie	BA	19	24	
Mealnek	Annie	BA	10	17	
Mechlinski	Adam J.	BA	10	11	
Mechlinski	Zacheuer	BA	2	17	
Mediecki	Simon	BA	19	15	
Meet	Fanny	BA	19	9	
Meidervriski	Joseph	BA	19	12	
Meinicke	Henry	BA	26	8	
Melczyn	Robert	BA	19	27	
Melenko	Steaf	BA	19	31	
Melerski	Anna	BA	19	4	
Meloniz	Frank	BA	19	30	
Memmes	Julius	BC	48	13	
Merkie	James	AA	17	12b	
Merriben	Joseph	BA	15	7	
Mesklosky	Thomas	BA	35	14	
Meyhchkya	Walter	BA	26	12	
Mgrarek	Thomas	BA	19	16	
Michalewski	Sigmund	BA	18	8	
Michalovski	Kazmer	BA	1	7	
Michalski	Frank	BA	17	30	
Michalski	Frank	BA	24	3	2
Michalski	Michalina	BA	11	11	
Michalski	Stefan	BA	16	12	

Last	First	CO	ED	PAG
Michalsky	Frank	BC	48	14
Michalsky	John	AA	18	16
Michalsky	John	AA	18	18
Michibyaski	Mary	BA	19	8
Michiewicz	Pelagia	BA	40	6 7
Michlinski	Joseph	BA	26	10
Micholak	Martin	BA	2	13
Mick	John	BA	26	7
Mickowski	Rudolph	BA	18	8
Miczhski	James	BA	19	7
Miczynski	John	BA	11	6
Mieduszewski	Bronislaw	BA	18	9
Miedzianswoka	Joseph A.	BA	18	3
Miencikowski	Stanislaus	BA	11	3
Mierzwicki	George	BA	19	7
Miewiadony	Philip	BA	17	6
Mihalak	Antonina	BA	26	12
Mik	Andrew	BA	18	10
Mik	Isidor	BA	19	18
Mikolazko	Jan M.	BA	17	31
Mikulska	Josef	BA	2	13
Milcholwska	Adam	BA	25	7
Mileska	Joseph	BA	26	7
Mileski	Jacob	BA	24	1
Miletzki	Charles	BA	26	10
Milicz	Antonie	BA	21	3
Milinoski	Cypoluary	BA	35	20
Miller	Andrew	BA	14	2 2
Miller	Andy	BA	19	28
Miller	John	BA	1	18
Miller	Julie	BA	25	4
Miller	Michael	BA	19	1
Mimczyk	John	BA	8	8
Miriski	Frank	BA	26	19
Mirus	Adam	BA	40	610
Miscimiesky	Antony	BA	40	612
Mishkryski	Stanislay	BA	19	11
Mishnak	Carrie	BA	26	10
Misiora	Joseph	BA	15	13
Miskowitz	Victoria	BA	10	16
Mislinski	John	BA	17	7
Mitchel	Thomas	BA	3	10
Mitchell	Jacob	BA	19	13
Mlynawyk	Stanislaw	BA	17	34
Modrak	John	BA	2	12
Moehauski	William	BA	19	18
Mokejwski	Teofril	BA	1	15
Mokrajk	James	BA	11	3
Molnaus	Frank	BA	26	8
Monazynski	Leo	BA	16	4

Last	First	CO	ED	PAG
Monssky	Clara	BA	17	8
Moraski	Anthony	BA	22	8
Morasski	Teafilas	BC	44	28
Morawski	Andrew M.	BA	24	10
Morawski	Henry	BA	17	7
Morawski	Ignacy	BA	17	8
Morawski	John	BA	17	12
Morawski	Wladyslau	BA	19	8
Morawsky	Alexander S.	BA	10	24
Morinski	Michael	BA	19	32
Moritzki	Thomas	BA	26	7
Morkeski	Cazmir	BA	9	24
Moroski	Joseph	AA	16	17a
Morowski	Victoria	BA	18	6
Morzuska	Michael	BA	19	33
Moshnikowski	Stanislawa	BA	40	6 1
Moshnikowsky	Michael	BA	40	6 1
Mosovski	Michael	BC	48	11
Motschski	Peter	BA	19	4
Movish	John	BA	4	3
Mraka	Romem	BA	17	31
Mrosinski	Dominick	BA	17	37
Mrowczynski	William	BA	18	14
Mroz	John	BA	17	31
Mrozewski	John	BA	24	11
Mrozinski	Franczek	BA	17	35
Mrozinski	Michael	BA	18	11
Mroznski	Barbara	BA	17	33
Mullen	John	BA	4	6
Muncisryniski	Antonia	BA	19	35
Muniewsky	Pawel	BA	40	613
Muratrsky	Andrew	BA	40	6 4
Murawski	Anna	BA	26	10
Murgarnski	Andrew	BA	1	14
Murszalek	Sophie	BA	15	12
Murzejewski	John F.	BA	11	7
Muszanowski	Ludwika	BA	19	34
Musznowski	Michael F.	BA	16	12
Mutszolek	Bronislawa	BA	2	6
Muychalk	Valentine	BA	8	5
Myeski	Walter	BC	68	29
Mylewski	Joseph	BA	40	6 6
Myska	William	BA	17	7
Myskowski	Michael	BA	19	15
Myslinsky	Vawishon	AA	18	12
Nachulski	Anna	BA	19	4
Nacoski	Joseph G.	BC	48	15
Nad--uski	Walter	BA	26	12
Nadoni	Alexander	BC	48	15
Nadulski	Agatha	BA	18	22

Last	First	CO	ED	PAG
Nagaka	Katarina	BA	21	4
Nagornowski	Brunon	BA	18	22
Nainsky	William	BC	46	25
Nairtski	Joseph	BC	68	29
Napastek	Michael	BA	17	3
Napavalski	Anna	BC	48	5
Napheski	Antoni	BA	26	9
Napiaralski	Joseph	BA	17	5
Napierkowski	Frank	BA	35	20
Napierski	Julian	BC	43	?
Napirala	Kaczimer	BA	17	30
Narinsky	Andy	BA	19	11
Narwosz	Cazmierz	BA	19	28
Nashowinski	Michael	BA	22	15
Nasuta	Elizabeth	BA	19	1
Nauricki	Josephine	BA	19	11
Naworski	Stephen	BA	16	5
Nawracki	Andrew	BA	18	14
Nawrozki	Joseph	BA	26	5
Naymon	Josephine	BA	26	10
Nelka	John M.	BA	2	7
Nelka	Maruna	BA	19	33
Nelska	Fransczk	BA	1	12
Nering	Poiter	BA	21	4
Neryngowski	Martin	BA	18	5
Niczks	Joseph	BA	40	6 4
Niedbalek	Michael	BA	26	3
Niedzielsky	Stanislaw	BA	40	610
Niedzwiecki	Casmer	BA	19	12
Niemczek	Andrew	BA	19	27
Niewadowski	Michael	BA	3	20
Niewiadowska	Rosie	BA	40	614
Nilka	Thomas	AA	16	1b
Nitka	Baltuni	BA	40	6 4
Nitschkowski	Eugene	BA	4	1
Nodolny	Adam	BA	3	37
Nodolsky	Peter	BA	40	6 4
Nolastek	Martin F.	BA	16	4
Noparstek	Dora	BA	3	8
Norcuski	Antone	BA	35	16
Nordonski	James	BA	3	8
Norgal	John	BA	22	16
Norisic	Peter	BA	2	10
Nortman	Mary	AA	16	17a
Norvaki	Jaskwas	BA	26	7
Norvich	August	BA	26	9
Nosal	Joseph	BA	35	19
Nosek	James	BA	1	12
Novak	August	BA	26	3
Novak	Edward	BA	19	18

Last	First	CO	ED	PAG
Novak	Irene	BA	18	7
Novak	Martin	BA	16	2
Novak	Michael	BA	8	7
Novak	Peter	BA	15	9
Novak	Peter	BA	18	8
Novak	Peter P.	BA	18	1
Novakosky	Wladislow	AA	18	18
Novakowski	Casmar J.	BC	48	14
Novecinskie	Wanston	AA	17	13b
Novitnski	Walter	BA	2	16
Novocinskie	Peter	AA	17	13a
Novotny	Wenceslaus	BA	14	6 3
Novrzchauski	Walter	BA	19	31
Novyzmska	Joseph	BA	19	8
Nowacki	Adam	BA	18	19
Nowacki	Ignacy	BA	18	19
Nowak	Alberta	BA	8	5
Nowak	Antonie	BA	17	37
Nowak	Baltazar	BA	18	6
Nowak	Casper	BA	4	4
Nowak	Cebbe	BA	17	33
Nowak	Ignacy	BA	19	13
Nowak	James	BA	17	24
Nowak	John	BA	15	11
Nowak	Joseph	BA	17	24
Nowak	Joseph	BA	17	35
Nowak	Joseph S.	BA	17	33
Nowak	Jozefee	BA	19	30
Nowak	Katiazyna	BA	40	6 4
Nowak	Ludyander	BA	19	13
Nowak	Martin	BA	19	27
Nowak	Michel	BA	15	9
Nowak	Stanislaw	BA	24	1
Nowak	Stansilaus	BA	19	7
Nowak	Stephen	BA	1	13
Nowak	Thomas	BA	11	7
Nowak	Valeria	AA	14	19a
Nowak	William	BA	17	26
Nowakewski	Andrew	BA	4	3
Nowakowska	Agnes	BA	24	6
Nowakowski	Antone	BA	15	13
Nowakowski	Frank	BA	17	24
Nowakowski	Frank	BA	9	5
Nowakowski	John	BA	17	13
Nowakowski	Joseph	BA	17	3
Nowakowski	Joseph	BA	5	16
Nowakowski	Szcsepan	BA	19	25
Nowakowski	Wladyslaw	BA	17	24
Nowitzka	Frank	BA	17	22
Nuska	John	BA	26	13

Last	First	CO	ED	PAG
Nuwodowski	Wenthy	BA	19	12
Nyklus	Bartlomies	BA	2	12
Nytha	Maricy	BA	22	16
Obojski	Alexander	BA	19	35
Oboncpak	Stumac	BC	49	13
Ochab	Andrew	BA	18	1
Oitiex	John	BA	19	8
Okoniczka	Michel	BA	17	30
Okonski	Andrew	BA	8	7
Okuniewsky	John	BA	40	6 5
Olaniski	Wladistaw	BA	26	1
Olek	Bawel	BA	17	35
Olek	Mikolay	BA	17	35
Olendrowicz	Felix	BA	16	10
Olenik	Julius	BA	14	2 2
Oles	Alexander	BA	19	14
Oles	Anthony	BA	5	14
Oles	Frank	BA	35	19
Oles	Jacob	BA	5	17
Oles	Joseph	BA	5	21
Oles	Peter	BA	8	7
Olezewski	Michal	BA	16	9
Olies	Pauline	BA	17	33
Oljewski	John	BA	25	1
Olkofski	George	BA	26	14
Olkoski	Michael	BA	17	31
Olschinsky	John	BC	65	12
Olshewska	Mary	BA	17	19
Olshewski	Antoni	BA	17	12
Olshiskie	John	AA	17	9a
Olski	James	BA	19	2
Olsyski	Thomas	BA	19	2
Olszewski	August	BA	19	6
Olszewski	Joseph	BA	19	25
Olszewski	Joseph	BC	43	?
Olszewski	Michael	BA	25	5
Olszewski	Peter	BA	19	24
Olszewsky	John	BA	40	610
Olszewsky	Stanislaw	BA	40	6 7
Olszewsky	Wladislaw	BA	40	6 7
Oltman	Maggie	BA	18	23
Olyniesak	M. Ambrose	BA	19	13
Onoziski	Martin	BC	55	18
Ordakowski	Frantz	BA	14	11
Ordaskowka	Teleska	BA	19	5
Orlefaski	William	BA	14	2
Orlekowski	Joseph	BA	19	17
Orloski	Edward	BA	19	25
Orlowska	Rose	BA	17	11
Orlowski	Lottie	BA	19	18

Last	First.	CO	ED	PAG
Ornstein	Henry	BA	19	5
Oronski	Walter	BA	26	9
Orowczynski	Frank	BA	11	7
Ortocki	Stanislaus	BA	35	4
Ortowsky	Romildt	BC	46	17
Orzakowski	Frances	BA	19	24
Osowsky	Stefan	BA	40	6 6
Ostazowski	John	BA	18	14
Ostrosky	Frank	AA	18	18
Ostrosky	Michael	BA	22	3
Ostrowski	Anton	BA	18	14
Ostrowski	Henry	BC	51	11
Ostrowski	John	BA	19	22
Ostrowsky	John	BA	40	6 3
Osuch	John	BA	5	23
Oszakiewski	William	BA	40	610
Oszewich	Jerome	AA	18	18
Osziendek	John	BA	18	10
Oszokowsky	August	BA	40	610
Otrombe	Maria	BA	19	16
Ott	William	BA	4	6
Ottman	Frank	BA	14	10
Owczerzak	Joseph	BA	40	6 4
Owozaczak	John	BA	11	1
Oyzinek	Verona	BA	17	16
Ozacky	Szymon	BA	40	6 5
Ozga	Agatia	BA	18	3·
Ozimek	Paul	BA	8	5
Pabich	Peter	BC	68	23
Pabyski	Henry	BA	35	17
Pac	Frank	BA	25	5
Pacholski	Vincent	BA	17	10
Paczanowski	Maryanna	BA	17	33
Padrossia	Joseph	BA	5	22
Page	Frank	BC	48	10
Paibalski	Jakob	BA	15	4
Pakarski	Jacob	BA	1	17
Pakowtzka	Adam	BC	48	7
Pakulski	Anna	BA	2	18
Pakulski	Joseph	BA	8	7
Pakulski	Stephen	BA	8	14
Palasik	Frank	BA	14	14
Palasik	John A.	BA	26	4
Palaszek	Wincent	BA	40	613
Palewicz	George	BA	2	17
Palucka	Katherine	BA	22	16
Panes	Peter	BA	19	26
Panis	John	BC	48	10
Panjewski	Charles	BA	25	8
Pansack	Catherine	BA	25	15

Last	First	CO	ED	PAG
Panushawski	Jan	BA	17	17
Papierniak	Fred	AA	7	?
Paptewski	John	BA	17	19
Parczynski	Sophie	BA	15	5
Paremski	John	BC	48	23
Parimski	Joseph	BA	10	20
Parinski	Frank	BA	19	9
Parinski	Louis	BA	26	13
Paryns	Adam	BC	48	10
Pasela	Jacob	BA	40	6 5
Pasint	Stephina	BA	5	12
Paska	Harry	BA	1	13
Paskow	Frank	BA	17	25
Pasnsna	Stanislaw	BA	17	26
Pasternak	William	BA	69	10
Pasternik	John	BA	40	611
Paszke	Jacob	BA	19	17
Paszkewich	Frank	AA	18	19
Paszkiewicz	Michael	BA	40	6 6
Patarski	John	BA	26	13
Patasik	Watesky	BA	16	1
Patelsky	Andrew	BA	8	7
Patro	George	BA	8	7
Paulukofsky	William J.	AA	18	6b
Pawaski	Edward	BA	18	7
Pawelcyk	Thomas	BA	26	3
Pawlak	Andrew	BA	19	30
Pawlak	Frances	BA	5	13
Pawlak	Frank A.	BA	24	5
Pawlak	Helena	BA	19	28
Pawlak	James	BA	19	13
Pawlak	John P.	BA	22	3
Pawlak	Josef	BA	19	20
Pawlak	Peter	BA	17	13
Pawlik	Stanislw	BA	2	10
Pawlofski	Peter	BA	35	16
Pawtanski	Stanislaw	BA	18	19
Pczydyzceski	Antonina	BA	17	35
Peans	James	BA	19	1
Peianowski	Michael	BA	17	31
Pelczar	Michael	BA	9	12
Peltz	John	AA	18	13
Peltz	Marcin	BA	8	9
Pencak	Mary	BA	3	21
Penewfsky	Zegmond	AA	18	16
Pensiorz	Frank	BA	8	7
Perkowski	Joseph	BA	17	31
Peszozynska	Anton	BC	42	12
Peteorski	Annie	BA	26	10
Petroski	Theodore	BA	26	3

Last	First	CO	ED	PAG
Petrosky	Frank	BC	48	14
Petrosska	Kasimer	BA	15	7
Petrowicz	Joe	BA	17	19
Petrowitz	Stanislaus	BA	17	24
Petshotski	Mike	BA	26	6
Pezwol	John	BA	17	33
Pfifer	Yan	BA	17	33
Pichoetski	William	BA	26	6
Pichowski	Helen	BA	18	8
Pick	Frank	BA	26	9
Picrol	Joseph	BA	14	6
Picuta	Katerzyna	BA	40	611
Piechoski	Marcin	BA	11	5
Piekarczyk	Thomas	BA	26	4
Pierginski	William	BA	26	10
Pieshaska	Joseph	BA	19	20
Pietnak	Casemer	BA	3	2
Pietrick	John	BA	26	7
Pietrok	Joseph	BA	4	1
Pietronska	Michael	BA	35	19
Pietrowiak	Josef	BA	2	13
Pietrowiak	Marcin	BA	8	9
Pietrowicak	John	BA	19	6
Piezczynski	Stanislaw	BA	18	8
Pilachowski	John	BA	4	2
Pilarski	Andrew J.	BA	1	17
Pilarski	Angelica	BA	19	13
Pilarski	Jan	BA	17	34
Pilarski	Joseph	BA	35	18
Pilashowsky	Frank	BA	40	6 8
Pilawski	Caszmer	BA	1	13
Piluch	Frank	BA	26	5
Piluk	John	BA	17	28
Pilzak	Victor	BA	26	9
Pinchnikowski	Lukas	BA	17	26
Pinchsoski	Joseph	BA	17	22
Pinchuerski	Felix	BA	16	8
Pininski	William	BA	19	9
Pinkoski	Joseph	BA	26	3
Pinkowski	Joseph	BA	17	25
Pinneski	Henry	BA	17	35
Pinnicki	Peter	BA	10	14
Piorinski	Ben	BA	17	7
Piornoski	Michael	BA	18	14
Piowinski	William	BA	17	7
Piowtkowsky	Anna	BA	40	612
Pis	Antonio	BA	2	13
Pisarek	Trzeslaw	BA	40	6 8
Pisarsky	Stanislaus	BA	9	4
Piscon	John	BA	26	8

Last	First	CO	ED	PAG
Piscor	Mary	BC	48	14
Piscor	Michael	BA	18	5
Piskarski	Alexandra	BA	17	5
Piskor	John	BA	17	11
Piskor	John	BA	17	26
Piskor	Joseph	BA	17	11
Piskor	Michael	BA	19	34
Piskor	Wojsuch	BA	19	17
Piszczako	Andrew	BA	69	10
Pitel	Henry	BA	17	31
Pitza	Joseph	BA	19	1
Platt	Louis P.	BA	18	22
Plewa	Wojciech	BA	8	6
Plewacka	Joseph	BA	8	8
Plewacki	Stanislaus	BA	6	8
Plewacki	Thomas	BC	44	17
Plichta	Frank	BA	40	6 7
Ploachvex	Paul	BA	19	2
Plotzak	Joseph	BA	17	27
Pluchta	Thomas	BA	16	3
Pluciak	Frank P.	BA	10	23
Plucinski	Agness	BA	5	14
Plum	Andrew P.	BA	18	1
Plum	Joseph S.	BA	18	4
Plusinski	Peter C.	BA	22	17
Pnocian	Feliks	BA	17	21
Pobocki	Maryana	BA	35	17
Pochoricka	George	BA	26	11
Podoski	John	BA	15	10
Poffel	Michael	BA	18	19
Poffel	Steny	BA	35	4
Pogelski	Stephan	BA	19	11
Pointkowski	Anton	BA	8	5
Pokorvki	Mary	AA	14	6a
Pokrywka	Paul	BA	19	3
Polak	Thomas	BA	17	8
Polanowski	Sigman	BA	18	14
Polasheck	Victor	BC	45	4
Polczynske	Maltaus	BA	26	19
Polek	Agnes	BA	17	26
Polek	Michal	BA	35	15
Polek	Szymon	BA	9	16
Polich	Frank	BA	35	14
Polik	Peter M.	BA	9	12
Polinski	John	BA	19	29
Polislack	Igniski	BA	19	5
Politowicz	Martin	BA	15	10
Politowski	John	BA	19	29
Polkowski	James	BA	3	8
Pollack	Louise	BA	9	26

Last	First	CO	ED	PAG	
Polonowicz	Stephen	BA	2	17	
Poluchowski	Alexander	BA	2	17	
Poluczinska	Macey	BA	3	7	
Polydras	Henry	BA	16	3	
Pomatowski	Bronislaw	BA	17	26	
Ponds	Frank	BA	26	13	
Ponds	Petronela	BA	26	7	
Popiel	Joseph	BA	19	29	
Popiotek	Stanislau	BA	19	5	
Popnacky	Joseph	BA	9	8	
Popowick	Wladislow	AA	18	18	
Popowski	Peter	BA	19	25	
Popuski	Ludwik	BA	19	24	
Porcheska	Andrew	BA	26	10	
Poremski	Matus	AA	13	12	
Porenski	Frank	BA	18	22	
Portankiewicz	Ignacy	BA	18	5	
Porulewski	John	BA	17	31	
Porzki	Tomaz	BA	19	33	
Posnaniak	Martin	BA	8	11	
Postanowicz	Roch	BA	26	4	
Postuszny	Wadyslaw	BA	19	20	
Poswiatowski	Charles	BC	48	11	
Poszko	Henry	BA	17	21	
Potaskiewicz	Walter	BA	17	33	
Poteraj	Stephen	BA	5	21	
Potocki	Stephen	BA	9	13	
Potonralska	Michel	BA	17	26	
Potroki	James	BA	26	9	
Potrsysky	Leon	BA	40	6	2
Potrzuski	Frank	BA	21	7	
Potter	Joseph	BA	2	17	
Potuyanski	Michail	AA	5	5	
Potzalska	Jacob	BA	3	10	
Poveroski	Alexander	BA	26	13	
Povinski	Lawrence	BA	19	10	
Powlak	Martin	BA	19	13	
Pozenski	Wojciech	BA	18	10	
Pozniak	William	BA	7	28	
Pozybylowski	Wladyslaw	BA	17	34	
Pragowski	Michael	BA	11	7	
Prenifskie	Mikel	AA	17	4b	
Prentki	Frank	BA	40	6	2
Preturyki	Tomasz	BA	19	32	
Price	John	BA	1	15	
Prichocki	John J.	BA	19	13	
Prijs	Annie	BA	9	8	
Pril	John	BA	40	6	5
Prizbylski	Michael	BA	17	10	
Prodakowski	Adolph	BA	17	18	

Last	First	CO	ED	PAG
Proseski	Helen	BA	1	16
Prosybylska	Frances	BA	26	8
Prothniki	Frank	BA	26	18
Protopski	John	BA	9	16
Protrsewitz	Piotr	BA	17	27
Prozniesky	Frank	BA	40	610
Prsybyle	John	BA	11	7
Pruchniecka	Catherine	BA	40	6 9
Pruchniewski	Valent	BA	17	13
Prusterowicz	John	BA	17	19
Prydyziewski	Joseph	BA	17	28
Pryzbulski	Frank	BA	10	24
Przybilski	Frank	BA	16	8
Przybis	Antonia	BA	40	614
Przybylski	John	BA	2	16
Przybylski	John	BA	26	2
Przybylski	Michael	BA	9	8
Przybylski	Stanislaw	BA	19	5
Przybzlski	Joseph	BA	1	16
Przyleylski	Joseph A.	BA	2	12
Przylsyewski	Mateusz	BA	19	16
Psczhnewski	Michael	BA	19	31
Ptotosyk Vincent	BA 3 20			
Ptussysky	Marczys	BA	40	612
Pubalski	Woliryan	BA	15	4
Puc	Anton	BA	17	16
Puczyski	Anton	BA	18	22
Pug	Frank	BA	26	6
Pukalski	Joseph	BA	17	21
Pula	Cunegunda E.	BA	35	19
Pural	William	BA	19	13
Putawski	Michael	BA	18	21
Puza	Andrew	BA	40	611
Puzycki	Peter	BA	35	20
Pyes	John	BA	40	613
Pygnas	Francis	BA	19	12
Pykaegowski	Ignac	BA	19	29
Pzerothoski	John	BA	15	10
Rabbitt	John	BA	5	23
Rachel	John	BA	17	37
Rachl	Wojcach	BA	19	11
Rachowski	Kasmier	BA	18	20
Rachuba	Joseph R.	BA	18	7
Rachuba	Marcel	BA	40	6 2
Rachubirski	Michael	BA	21	3
Raczkiemoz	Joseph	BA	3	2
Raczniak	John	BA	5	22
Radecki	Jakub	BA	2	7
Radishowsky	John	AA	18	9
Radowka	Teresa	BA	9	6

Last	First	CO	ED	PAG	
Rafunski	Roman	BA	2	11	
Raguski	Wladislaw	BA	1	14	
Rahoba	Angela	BA	26	9	
Rajisky	Andy	BA	19	5	
Rak	John	BA	17	3	
Rakowicz	Wladyslaw	BA	2	18	
Rakowski	Viola	BA	26	7	
Rakowski	Vola	BA	26	7	
Rakowsky	Adolph	BA	40	6	2
Ralajezak	Michael	BA	1	15	
Ramus	August R.	BA	3	10	
Ras	Joseph	BA	26	8	
Rastsky	Frank	BA	17	24	
Raszeja	Joseph A.	BA	18	9	
Rataczak	Thomas	BA	4	2	
Rataczyk	John	BA	17	33	
Ratajcyak	Andrew	BA	2	12	
Ratazak	Anthony J.	BA	5	23	
Ratoyczak	Henry	BA	11	11	
Ratszezek	Michael	BA	19	29	
Ratyczak	Michael	BA	9	6	
Rawa	Antone	BA	15	8	
Rawicki	Joseph	BA	26	9	
Rawinic	John	BA	17	26	
Rayzhal	Wojcach	BA	19	33	
Razynski	Aitor	BA	17	19	
Rdowsky	Frank	BC	68	29	
Rebetskie	Joseph	AA	17	11a	
Rebrowski	John	BA	17	30	
Rechuba	Andrew	BA	19	29	
Recka	Mary	BA	8	7	
Reczensky	Bronislaw	BA	40	6	9
Rednick	Janina	BA	17	16	
Redzensky	Antony	BA	40	6	8
Regulska	Thomas	BA	9	2	
Reinbic	Christopher	BA	19	5	
Rejski	James	BA	2	20	
Rekiel	Walter	BA	18	15	
Rembis	Agnes	BA	40	6	5
Rendczilski	Helena	BA	17	30	
Renik	Joseph	BA	4	1	
Renkowska	Sophia	BA	40	6	6
Reocaja	Anton	AA	13	3	
Reosthski	Frank	BA	1	14	
Retajezsak	Joseph	BA	1	13	
Retchiak	William	AA	12	7	
Retowsky	James	BC	45	15	
Rettkowski	William	BC	48	13	
Reves	Mikel	AA	17	9a	
Rewes	Frank	BA	16	11	

Last	First	CO	ED	PAG
Ribicky	Stanislaw	BA	40	610
Rice	John	BA	17	27
Richmezolski	Stanolau	BA	1	12
Richter	Joseph	BA	40	6 7
Rikowski	Ignacy	BA	17	34
Riluk	Joseph	BA	17	19
Ritka	Wincenty	BA	16	10
Rochowiak	Michael	BA	8	5
Rochowicz	Joseph	BA	10	20
Rocklitz	Christian	AA	9	5
Rocufskie	Nellie	AA	17	13a
Roebanski	Henry	BA	9	2
Roesthski	Frank	BA	1	13
Rogowsky	Dominek	BA	40	6 2
Rogza	Walenti	BA	19	10
Rohski	Joseph	BA	18	16
Rokold	Frank	AA	17	13b
Rolak	Edward	BA	26	4
Roluski	Stefana	BA	1	41
Roman	Walenty	BA	18	13
Romano	John	BA	19	28
Rominski	Joseph	BA	18	9
Rominsky	Casmier	BA	18	18
Ropanski	Anthony	BC	44	24
Ropinskie	Bronstow	AA	17	9a
Roploski	Joseph	BA	3	21
Rorbownczka	Pahel	BA	19	1
Roscielski	Frank R.	BA	18	10
Rose	Sister	BA	17	17
Rosiak	Julian	BA	18	22
Rosiak	Stanislaw	BA	18	22
Rosinska	Mary	BA	18	4
Rosinski	Stanisllaus	BA	2	17
Rosnowski	Stanislaw	BA	18	8
Rossalek	Joseph	BA	19	12
Rostek	Wladyslaw	BA	17	28
Rostkowski	Edward	BA	15	10
Rosunonufski	Joseph	AA	17	9b
Roswska	Frank	BA	1	16
Roszyk	Michael	BA	8	10
Roulski	Stefana	BA	2	7
Rowalewski	Joseph	BA	26	6
Rozmus	Anna	BA	5	22
Roznamak	Frank	BA	8	11
Rudmicki	Antoni	BA	17	10
Rudzinski	Frank	BA	18	23
Rudzynski	Adam	BA	14	11
Rulance	Alexander	BC	48	15
Rull	Adam	AA	17	8b
Rulski	Marie	BA	24	1

Last	First	CO	ED	PAG
Rumanski	Peter	BA	1	15
Rumbrowski	Joseph	BA	17	28
Rumbunck	Annie	BA	19	9
Runanski	Peter	BA	19	14
Rusakey	Michael	BA	1	16
Ruschinyki	Mary	BA	19	4
Rushang	William	BA	19	4
Rusin	Fulryel	BA	16	3
Rusin	Jozefa	BA	16	1
Rusinsky	Andrew	BA	19	10
Ruska	Frank	BA	9	24
Ruski	James	BA	18	14
Russel	Adam	AA	18	18
Rusty	Pawel	BA	17	12
Ruszke	Vincent	BA	17	19
Rutkauski	Joseph	BA	19	28
Rutkauski	Koven	BC	68	27
Rutkowski	Anton	BA	18	6
Rutkowski	Florjan	BA	19	16
Rutkowski	Joseph	BA	17	7
Rutkowski	Stanislaw	BA	19	20
Rutkowsky	Paul	BA	40	613
Rutschska	Joseph	BA	16	2
Ruzakowski	Adam	BA	17	21
Ruzminski	Casemer	BA	19	14
Rybaciak	John	BA	18	12
Rybacosyk	Victoria	BA	18	12
Rybarczyk	Cassimia	BA	4	3
Rybicki	Mary	BA	19	34
Rybrick	Martin	BA	19	31
Rycharski	Joseph	BA	16	9
Rychwalski	Andy	BA	19	5
Rychwalski	Antoni	BA	19	7
Rychwska	Charles	BA	16	5
Rydsiewski	Bromistaw	BA	17	17
Rydtiska	Melanicka	BC	48	2
Rydzewski	Walter	BA	17	5
Rykaczinoski	Cornell	BA	17	6
Rylarczk	Frank	BA	19	4
Rylarczsyki	Stella	BA	19	15
Rymas	Wladyslaw	BA	17	14
Rymiewicz	Charles	BA	19	8
Ryshkiewicz	Adam	BA	17	11
Rytel	John	BA	17	1
Rzczyk	Tomas	BA	40	6 3
Rzrpka	Francis	BA	3	2
Rzydzinski	John	BA	8	7
Sabolefsky	John	AA	18	4
Saboroski	John	BA	4	4
Sacrosinski	Frank	BA	25	7

Last	First	CO	ED	PAG
Sadfosky	William	BC	55	18
Sadinchiski	Alex	BA	19	11
Sadler	Andrew	BC	66	15
Sadler	John	BC	48	14
Sadowski	Joseph	BA	25	15
Sadowski	Mary R.	BA	19	29
Sadowski	Michael F.	BA	19	30
Sadowski	Vincent	BA	19	16
Sadowski	Wiktor	BA	16	4
Sadowsky	Frank	BA	40	6 7
Saffeta	Frank	BA	2	7
Safroski	Kazimer	BA	1	12
Saircki	Mike	BA	26	3
Sakalowisky	Joseph	AA	18	3
Sakosky	John	BA	52	13
Salarski	Andrew	AA	17	12b
Salinski	Annie	BA	17	5
Salschoska	Helena	BA	40	6 2
Samlanski	Frank	BA	1	18
Sanduskey	August	BC	7	11
Sanfert	George	BA	11	9
Sansaskie	Annie	AA	17	13a
Sasiadek	Thomas	BA	26	10
Sass	James	AA	13	3
Sass	Jozef	BA	16	10
Satowski	Alex	BA	19	29
Sawicki	Andrew	BA	2	17
Sawicky	Adolph	BA	40	6 3
Sawitzki	George	BA	25	17
Sawoski	Frank	BA	26	19
Sawosky	Joseph	BA	40	6 2
Sawska	Andrew	BA	1	13
Sawski	Marian	BC	48	15
Sceszek	Martin	BA	17	21
Schab	John	BA	17	25
Schaffer	Casimir	BA	19	9
Schalaski	Anna	BA	21	3
Schelecki	Kate	BA	19	11
Scheninski	Eugene	BA	26	4
Schieaer	John	BA	24	6
Schilkski	Cazmir	BA	19	3
Schinewski	Michael	BA	19	33
Schlind	George	BA	10	16
Schlistke	John	BA	26	6
Schmidt	Anna	BA	19	33
Schminschski	Frank	BA	19	8
Schminski	Andy	BA	19	29
Schroeder	Michael	BA	22	17
Schrowinski	Adelbert	BA	19	5
Schudwjcheska	John	BA	19	8

Last	First	CO	ED	PAG
Schultz	Adam	BA	1	17
Schultz	Anton	BA	21	4
Schultz	Frank	BA	16	7
Schultz	Frank	BA	26	12
Schultz	Frank R.	BA	26	14
Schultz	Joseph	BA	18	10
Schultz	Martin	BA	25	7
Schulz	Vicenty	BA	40	612
Schulze	Frank	BA	17	18
Schuwalski	George	BA	20	6 2
Schwartz	Steven	BA	22	16
Schybilski	Joseph	BA	26	12
Schymoshik	Martin	BA	26	10
Sckovowica	Antonie	BC	44	12
Sctultz	Frank	BA	21	10
Scyamanski	John	BA	26	9
Sczegowski	Adam	BA	16	11
Sczepaniak	Joseph	BA	17	21
Sczepaniak	Pioter W.	BA	17	26
Sczepanski	Martin	BA	21	4
Sczepansky	Stanislow	AA	18	9
Sealock	Joseph	AA	18	24
Sebatka	Adam	BA	26	4
Sebinskie	John	AA	17	13b
Sebrowski	Adam	BA	17	25
Seglinski	Catherine	BA	6	7
Seglinski	John C.	BA	8	9
Seibel	John	BA	90	21
Selinski	Joseph	BA	9	8
Seofoka	John	BA	26	13
Sepanski	Martin	BC	66	15
Serek	Andrew	BA	18	22
Setelki	Frank	BA	19	7
Setera	Martin	BA	25	1
Seteski	David	BA	17	31
Setlak	James	BA	19	10
Sevinsky	Frank	BA	1	13
Sewitzski	George	BA	25	1
Seyerski	Boleslaw	BA	17	30
Sgewe	Francis	BA	1	15
Shabelski	Louis	BA	17	12
Shafer	Fronia	BA	26	6
Shafranski	Antonina	BA	17	6
Shalkolsky	Gustaw	AA	18	4
Shalsky	Henry	BA	26	1
Shank	Peter	BA	26	12
Shazepanski	Kiel	BA	17	7
Shazepanski	Walerian	BA	17	16
Shicelisky	Steve	AA	18	7
Shilasky	Charles	AA	21	14

Last	First	CO	ED	PAG
Shinskey	Adam	BC	55	8
Shipukiewicz	Lawrence	BA	17	1
Shizmanski	John	BA	17	15
Shmikowski	Stanislaus	BA	19	14
Shomsky	Joseph	AA	18	4
Shorts	Eke	BC	51	12
Shubeck	Joseph	AA	16	1b
Shultesky	George	BA	2	7
Shultz	Andy	BA	19	31
Shurinski	Pawel	BA	17	28
Shymansky	Edward	BA	6	3
Shymborska	Mary	BA	17	12
Sibiska	Alexander	BC	44	12
Sibiski	John	BC	44	28
Sibistowicz	Frank	BA	15	13
Siblewski	Michael	BA	13	9
Sibstowicz	Karol	BA	3	6
Sickora	Joseph	BA	17	31
Sieber	?	BA	16	7
Siedlecki	Alex R.	BA	24	1
Siegmund	John, Sr.	BA	11	12
Siegmunt	James	BA	8	9
Siejak	Alexander	BC	48	2
Siekierki	Frank	BC	42	1
Siekierski	Martin	BA	5	17
Siemanski	George	BA	19	12
Sienkiewicz	Wincenty	BA	40	6 2
Sierak	Antoni	BA	16	12
Siewierski	Peter M.	BA	18	6
Siewierski	Roman	BA	19	7
Siewiski	Sophia	BA	2	10
Sigai	Frank	BA	5	16
Sikes	John	BA	25	17
Sikoski	Victor	BA	18	8
Sikowski	John	BA	22	11
Simanok	Gim	AA	18	2
Siminski	Matthew	BA	2	13
Simmins	Frank	BA	1	16
Simmons	Charles	BA	8	1
Simon	Anastazy	BA	14	2
Simon	Joseph	BA	19	3
Sinetowski	Joseph	BA	15	10
Sinskey	Arthur	BC	55	8
Sinski	Lawrence	BA	17	7
Sinsky	Catherine	BA	14	17
Sisiecki	Charles K.	BA	11	1
Sito	Robert	BA	26	14
Siwierski	Joseph	BA	2	6
Siwinski	George W.L.	BA	18	4
Siwinski	Walter B.	BA	18	22

Last	First	CO	ED	PAG
Skalinsky	Frak	BA	40	610
Skalinsky	Teophil	BA	40	611
Skalska	Veroneka	BA	2	6
Skarbex	Jasenty	BA	17	3
Skelvinski	John	BA	26	6
Sklodowski	Browislaw	BA	15	10
Skoccynaski	Annie	BA	9	4
Skoturski	Martin S.	BA	22	7
Skraupa	Francis	BA	19	27
Skraupa	Wincenty	BA	19	27
Skroch	Mathews	BA	17	10
Skrydlewski	Woinech	BA	17	33
Skrzynski	Jaruza W.	BA	19	9
Skwinut	Tadesuz	BA	26	5
Skworski	George	BA	19	28
Skynski	Christinia	BA	21	11
Slanski	John	BA	11	7
Slaska	Frank	BA	8	11
Slaska	Teofil	BA	21	7
Slawinska	Stephan	BA	1	18
Slawska	Julja	BA	17	19
Slebioda	Michael	BA	2	12
Sleclenski	Ignatz	BA	17	22
Slewka	Alexander	BA	18	10
Sleyewski	Sophia	BA	9	8
Sliminski	John S.	BA	18	16
Slipski	Andrew	BA	17	5
Slowick	John	BA	6	7
Slowik	Felix	BA	18	18
Slowrekurski	Josef	BA	19	14
Sluzewski	Frank	BA	18	15
Sluzewski	John S.	BA	26	8
Smialek	Francis	BA	18	13
Smiglawski	Leonard	BA	1	186
Smiglawski	Sophia	BA	9	6
Smith	Agness	AA	17	15
Smith	Franciska	BA	15	8
Smith	Martin F.	BA	15	7
Smolenska	Bronistawa	BA	24	1
Smolinski	Andrew	BA	2	16
Smolinski	August	BA	19	3
Smolinski	Joseph	BA	8	1
Smoscufskie	Joseph	AA	17	9a
Smoykiuwiz	John	BC	48	23
Smyroski	William	BA	26	6
Sneciak	Walenty	BA	17	35
Sneigowska	Henry	BA	9	8
Sniegowski	Charles	BA	15	15
Sobezak	Martin	BA	13	9
Sobieski	Louis	BA	3	10

Last	First	CO	ED	PAG
Sobiloska	Dominic	BC	48	8
Sobolewski	Frank	BA	18	14
Sobolewski	John	BA	4	4
Sobolewski	John	BA	5	14
Sobotka	Antonina	BA	40	612
Sobousnski	Josef	BA	19	5
Soboz	George	BA	26	7
Sobus	Frank	BA	40	6 7
Sobus	Peter	BA	40	613
Sobusz	Leon	BA	40	6 4
Sobusz	Michael	BA	40	610
Socha	Joseph	BA	18	22
Socki	Antonie	BA	2	12
Sofnoka	Michael	BC	48	2
Sojka	Joseph	BA	19	4
Sojka	Stanislaw	BA	8	11
Sokewski	Stanislaw	BA	4	1
Solinski	Joseph	BC	65	12
Solinskie	Hypolyt	AA	17	13a
Soliskey	Joseph	BA	11	4
Solkowsky	Michael	BA	40	614
Soltys	Henry	BA	35	17
Soltzsiak	Anastza	BA	16	1
Sopczynski	Walenty	BA	17	32
Sopiskwy	George	BA	11	3
Sosnowsky	Marian	BA	40	6 9
Sosnowsky	Warzeniec	BA	40	6 9
Sottysiak	Peter J.	BA	19	4
Sowa	Eva	BA	8	5
Sowski	William	BA	17	12
Spak	Mark	BA	17	3
Spara	Frank	BA	40	613
Spedden	George	BC	48	2
Spinestowicz	Anna	BA	17	12
Spochaeq	Michael	BA	3	2
Spohucz	John	BA	16	4
Sporney	Julia	BA	22	7
Sporny	Frank	BA	21	3
Sporny	James W.	BA	18	20
Sporny	Martin	BA	17	19
Spring	Anna	BA	21	11
Square	Robert	BC	51	11
Srebna	Kosstancsyja	BA	2	12
Srebomiski	Andrea	BA	2	17
Srebomiski	Constanty	BA	2	17
Srendzewski	James	BA	26	19
Sroka	Mary	BA	26	5
Sroka	Mary S.	BA	6	1
Stacharowski	Lena	BA	19	5
Stachlelski	Ignatius	BA	26	19

Last	First	CO	ED	PAG
Stachowak	Mary	BA	19	9
Stachowicz	Joseph	BA	17	6
Stachowski	Andrew	BA	16	5
Stachowski	Frank	BC	66	15
Stachowski	John	BA	19	20
Stachowski	John	BC	68	29
Stackoski	Martin	BA	19	26
Stackowicz	Joseph	BA	17	5
Stackowski	Anthony	BA	5	21
Stackowski	Michal	BC	41	112
Stadarowski	Feliex	BA	14	17
Stadranowski	Felix	BA	15	17
Stadziki	Adam	BA	10	23
Stafafitza	Verla	BA	26	7
Staibovurch	Joseph	BA	15	7
Staka	Eva	BA	18	8
Stalczig	Felix	BA	17	28
Stamborski	Antonie	BA	17	34
Stamiec	Frank	BA	26	13
Stamiewicz	Peter	BA	24	10
Stanchiski	Mary	BA	19	5
Staniewski	Ignatz	BA	2	18
Staniewski	Lawrence	BA	14	1 7
Staniewski	Michael	BA	8	8
Staniewski	Peter	BA	2	17
Stanislaus	Stepen	BA	16	6
Stanislawski	Joseph	BA	3	7
Staniszewsky	Francis	BA	40	6 8
Stankowski	Frank	BA	19	7
Stankowski	Joseph	BA	11	7
Stankowsky	Stephan	BA	35	11
Stanosky	Edward	BA	14	2 2
Stanynski	Thomas	BA	17	1
Staplicky	Stephen	AA	18	18
Starzynski	John	BA	11	6
Starzynski	Joseph	BA	18	4
Stashalyski	Joseph	BA	16	4
Stasiak	Victoria	BA	16	8
Stasiak	William	BA	4	4
Staskowsak	Martin	BA	19	25
Staszak	Michael	BA	9	4
Stauzki	Anafly	BA	1	16
Stawinska	John	BA	5	17
Stefan	Mary	BA	5	14
Stefankiewicz	Valentine	BA	18	14
Stefanski	Ignatius T.	BA	2	6
Stefanski	Mary	BA	19	29
Stefanski	Matias	BA	18	6
Stefanski	Michael	BA	19	5
Stefanski	Raymond	BA	23	15

Last	First	CO	ED	PAG
Stefanski	Thomas	BA	4	5
Stefenski	I.	BA	19	5
Steffen	George	BA	2	13
Stein	Robert	BA	18	22
Stelmaszek	Frank	BA	40	6 5
Stemski	John	BA	18	5
Stepanski	Anton	BA	1	15
Stephanski	Michael	BA	6	18
Stetz	John	BA	8	10
Stewonski	Frank	BC	49	13
Steziska	John	BA	26	14
Sticzynski	Joseph P.	BA	8	8
Sticzynski	Martin	BA	8	8
Stocklinski	John	BA	26	16
Stoda	Andrew M.	BA	24	11
Stodena	Agnes	BA	17	30
Stofkoni	Gabriel	BC	48	9
Stojewsky	Antony	BA	40	612
Stokowski	Bolestar	BA	17	12
Stolinski	Alexander	BA	24	5
Stolinski	Michler	BA	15	9
Stolz	Sofia	BA	21	10
Stopczenski	Frank	BA	2	13
Stoskoski	Frank	BA	3	22
Stoteka	John	BA	1	15
Stowikowski	Teofil	BA	17	8
Strakalska	Feliska	BA	26	10
Strieska	Mary	BA	26	14
Stroginski	Carl	BA	26	5
Stromsky	Alexander	BC	51	13
Strosinski	Victor	BA	26	8
Strozyszkowski	Andy	BA	19	23
Strugala	Jacob	BA	5	19
Strunofsky	Stanislaw	BA	21	7
Strunsky	August	BC	55	18
Stryhusz	Stanislaus	BA	17	23
Strzegowski	Mikolay	BA	40	6 1
Strzelcik	Marcin	BA	5	19
Strzelewsky	Herman	BA	40	6 8
Stuazinska	John	BA	8	14
Stublewski	Andrew	BA	17	33
Stuctzinski	Charles	BA	24	3
Studzinski	John	BA	5	22
Studzinski	Mary M.	BA	26	8
Studzinski	Michael	BA	18	4
Stupenski	Annie	BA	9	8
Stuzensky	Walenty	BA	5	21
Stzneckski	Martin	BA	11	4
Subinska	Peter F.	BA	7	28
Suckofska	Sophia	BC	48	23

Last	First	CO	ED	PAG
Sudowski	Andy	BA	19	33
Sudowski	Frances	BA	19	17
Sudowski	John	BA	15	5
Suki	Joseph	BA	18	16
Sul	John	BA	40	612
Sulch	Antoni	BA	26	11
Sulowski	John	BA	17	25
Sumek	Andrzef	BA	8	9
Supuczynski	John J.	BA	17	34
Surncsznski	Wojciecu	BA	16	11
Surnowski	Antonie	BA	17	29
Suszynski	Andrew A.,Rev.	AA	18	20
Sutorski	James	BA	17	21
Suvak	John	BA	1	18
Suwalski	John M.	BA	24	3 2
Suwalski	Stephan	BA	18	1
Suwczensky	Stanislaw	BA	40	6 3
Suwlenski	Head	BA	26	19
Suzarzinski	Joseph	BA	15	12
Swanczyk	Peter	BA	8	9
Swanhoski	Martin	BC	65	12
Swcoski	William	BA	1	16
Swiderski	Antony	BA	21	10
Swiec	Andrew	BA	2	13
Swierski	Frank A.	BA	14	14
Swietoslawa	Mary, Sister	BA	17	17
Swigon	Kasper	BA	18	14
Swigty	Martin	BA	17	15
Swisk	Bessie	BA	19	13
Switkowska	Anna	BA	17	13
Swjateski	Andrew	BA	17	8
Sworecki	Martin	BA	18	14
Syckukauski	Apolinary	BA	19	24
Sycoski	Marion	BA	26	9
Sygmont	Jan	BA	19	6
Sylvazkski	Joseph	BA	16	4
Symborsky	Joseph	BA	40	6 6
Sypieska	Agnieska	BA	2	10
Szacheznski	Stamslus	BA	15	6
Szambursky	Teofil	AA	18	20
Szamski	Peter	BA	15	5
Szaska	Joseph	BA	40	612
Szatkowsky	Wojczech	BA	40	6 5
Szaworski	Aldys	BA	23	15
Szcerbicki	Frank	BA	18	15
Szczepanski	Alexander	BA	16	6
Szczepanski	Frank	BA	17	1
Szczepanski	Lawrence	BA	17	1
Szczeswik	Anton	BA	19	29
Szczurowski	Alexander	BA	19	25

Last	First	CO	ED	PAG	
Szczypinki	Frank	BA	35	23	
Szdebzki	Martin	BA	3	8	
Szeliga	Adam	BA	26	13	
Szemborski	Gus	BA	11	1	
Szerublewski	Frank	BA	15	13	
Szezerbicki	Peter	BA	18	15	
Szinski	John	BA	9	7	
Szlunczka	Tomas	BA	40	6	3
Szmare	Valentine	BA	9	3	
Szmencky	Daniel	BA	40	6	2
Szmiaki	Henry	BA	5	7	
Szok	Peter	BA	40	6	8
Szozech	Henry	BC	48	12	
Szpakowski	Nikonor	BA	2	17	
Szpolura	John	BA	40	6	4
Sztoda	Joseph	BA	11	7	
Szucknisky	Boleslaw	AA	18	16	
Szucknisky	Peter	AA	18	16	
Szwesecky	John	AA	18	13	
Szwinski	Harry	BA	11	1	
Szyczukowski	Ignacy	BA	18	16	
Szykowna	Victoria	BA	17	15	
Szymacki	Frank	BA	17	35	
Szymanowski	Frances	BA	26	2	
Szymanowski	Joseph	BA	18	4	
Szymanowski	Theodor	BA	26	2	
Szymanska	Mariana	BA	10	17	
Szymanski	Agnes	BA	34	3	
Szymanski	Andrew	BA	14	14	
Szymanski	John B.	BA	8	3	
Szymanski	Joseph	BA	26	9	
Szymanski	Leon	BA	19	11	
Szymanski	Michael	BA	19	29	
Szymanski	Michael	BA	19	6	
Szymanski	Peter	BA	22	16	
Szymanski	Rose	BA	16	1	
Szymanski	Walter	BA	18	16	
Szymansky	Joseph	BA	40	6	9
Szymansky	Michael	BA	40	6	9
Szymborski	John	BA	8	6	
Szymek	John	BA	17	3	
Szymiski	Anton	BA	19	25	
Szymkowiak	Antonia	BA	16	3	
Szymkowiak	John	BA	21	10	
Szymyewski	Stanislaus S.	BA	18	7	
Szymzowski	Mary	BA	19	22	
Szynkowak	Jacob	BA	1	7	
Szyzewski	Mary	BA	11	9	
Taback	Joseph	BA	4	1	
Tabula	Frederick	BA	17	31	

Last	First	CO	ED	PAG
Tachowski	Stanisla	BA	22	15
Tadayewski	John	BA	16	3
Tadowski	Clement	BA	3	6
Tarowiewska	Zofia	BA	19	11
Tatarwicz	Jacob	BA	2	17
Tatarwig	Stephen	BA	2	17
Tatutis	Kazimier	BA	16	3
Taylor	Henry	BA	19	1
Taylrs	Cecelia	BA	14	6
Teclaw	Ignacy	BA	16	3
Tedejefski	Michael	BA	25	15
Telakowicz	John	BA	19	23
Teller	Frank	BA	19	27
Telocleowki	Jan	BA	13	9
Tema	Mary	BA	10	16
Thailowicz	John	BA	17	16
Thomadu	Tillie	BA	35	19
Thwid	Wojciech	BA	17	5
Tichoruts	Joseph	BA	15	15
Tienkiewicz	John	BA	17	16
Ties	John	BC	48	15
Timbiewicz	Frank	BA	8	11
Tiskolski	James	BA	21	3
Tolodz	John	BA	18	16
Tomaliki	Thomas S.	BA	18	18
Tomashewski	Theodor	BA	17	12
Tomaszeski	Michal	BA	17	21
Tomaszewski	Dominican	BA	19	5
Tomaszewsky	Antony	BA	40	6 8
Tomenwski	Andrew	BC	48	8
Topkoski	Andrew	BA	2	18
Topolski	Waclaw	BA	2	8
Topolsky	Mary	BA	2	7
Torensky	Woetczek	AA	18	19
Toschenski	Alexander	BA	2	19
Traiaczewski	Henry	BA	17	33
Trajaunowiski	Joeseph	BA	26	12
Trawinski	Joseph F.	BA	26	5
Trawinsky	Maczy	BA	40	610
Trdski	Adam	BA	17	21
Treianowski	Joseph	BA	17	30
Trenicarski	Pelagia	BA	17	4
Trisczynsky	Jacob	BA	40	6 2
Tropczynski	Albert	BA	2	13
Trouth	Tofel	BA	18	8
Trovosky	Adolph	AA	19	4
Truczowski	Maria	BA	19	34
Trukaski	Frank	BA	2	16
Truskowski	Peter	BA	11	7
Truskowski	Wladysla	BA	15	9

Last	First	CO	ED	PAG
Trusskauski	Paul	BA	19	18
Truszcynski	Michat	BA	16	5
Truszkowska	Lenan	BA	40	611
Truszkowsky	Peter	BA	40	613
Trybulowski	Antoni	BA	2	6
Trygaj	Joseph W.	BA	1	14
Trzaska	Stanislaw	BA	40	612
Trzcciak	Catherine	BA	16	4
Trzciak	Andrew	BA	19	5
Trzczinski	Stanislaus	BA	18	14
Trzczynski	Stephan	BA	26	19
Trzomski	Vallenty	BA	25	4
Trzysky	Joseph	BA	40	6 8
Tucholka	Frank B.	BC	46	17
Tukauski	Mary	BA	19	32
Tukoszewski	Marryanna	BA	8	11
Tunjnska	Frances	BA	11	7
Turaczyk	Henry H.	BA	16	8
Turmak	Jacob	BA	8	5
Turow	Peter	BA	11	9
Twardouski	Marya	BA	35	18
Twardowicz	Peter S.	BA	18	13
Twardowski	Mateurs	BA	19	28
Twckaswska	Katie	BA	17	7
Tworek	Josephine	BA	40	611
Tycrykouski	Max	BA	19	15
Tyma	Frank G.	BA	15	5
Tyna	Joe	BA	19	32
Tyrpak	Makan	BA	40	6 4
Tysakiewicz	Felix	BA	19	2
Tyshmaki	Rose	BA	19	4
Tyski	Michael	BA	1	12
Tysko	Stansilus	BA	19	3
Tzalcer	Frank	BA	24	5
Tzlesucki	Kazimiera	BA	21	3
Ulamowicz	Stanislaus	BA	15	10
Ulenicka	Frances	AA	18	19
Uletowsky	Alexander	AA	18	16
Ulmanijawski	Mary A.	BA	5	12
Uminia	Sophia	BA	17	31
Uncik	Frank	BA	17	10
Urbacz	Franciska	BA	17	3
Urban	Joseph	BA	15	13
Urbanauski	Antonia	BA	19	32
Urbanowics	John	BA	3	21
Urbanowski	Franciszad	BA	19	32
Urbanowski	Frank	BA	19	32
Urbanski	John	BA	18	5
Urbanski	Michael	BA	19	28
Urbanski	Peter	BA	17	21

Last	First	CO	ED	PAG
Urbanski	Samuel	BA	17	24
Urbanski	Wadysaw	BA	3	21
Urbaynski	Anna	BA	17	35
Ustak	Victor	BA	26	11
Ustusgowsky	Frank	BA	40	6 4
Uzewski	James	BA	16	6
Vagerski	Frank	BA	26	14
Vagierski	Celia	BA	3	57
Valondek	Frank	BA	26	3
Vasakowski	Joseph	BA	35	11
Velepsky	Frank	BA	26	4
Velzant	Frances	BA	40	6 7
Velzant	Stanislaw	BA	40	6 7
Venechizki	Frank	BA	19	8
Viczek	Bronislow	AA	18	16
Vilicky	Stanislow	AA	18	3
Visniewski	Vicenty	BA	19	31
Vodack	Mary	BA	26	12
Voltner	Fred	BA	22	17
Voriesky	Paul	AA	18	16
Vozycka	Mary	BA	17	5
Vsent	Joseph	BA	26	7
Vuechitsky	John	AA	18	3
Vzeczinsky	Stanislow	AA	18	13
Wabinsky	John	BA	45	15
Wachacki	Stanislaw	BA	19	34
Wachjnski	Alexander	BA	19	7
Wachowiak	John	BA	17	5
Waclawsky	John	BA	17	25
Wacotorwski	Joseph	BA	3	20
Wacznek	Budnz	BA	19	16
Waczynski	Antone	AA	14	6a
Wadshaski	John	BA	16	3
Waewyzisak	Jacob	BA	19	13
Wagenska	Anna	BA	17	25
Waggay	Fetonia	BA	17	35
Wagner	John	BA	19	25
Wagner	Thomas	BA	21	7
Wahowiak	Katarzyna	BA	16	6
Wajek	Dora	BA	17	12
Wakowiak	Peter	BA	17	22
Walazewski	Lizzie	BA	1	16
Walbusky	Frank	AA	15	7b
Walcuk	Edward	BA	19	18
Walecki	Piort	BA	18	6
Wales	Wojciech	BA	16	11
Walkowiak	John	BA	8	6
Walkowiak	Vincent	BA	8	9
Wallace	Adam	BA	3	10
Wallas	Mary	BA	10	11

Last	First	CO	ED	PAG	
Walters	John	BA	70	3	
Walzierski	John	BA	19	8	
Wanar	Marton	BA	40	6	4
Wanchansuski	Alex	BA	19	7	
Wancowicz	Kazmier	BA	40	614	
Waniak	Andrew	BA	16	12	
Wankowsky	Wladislow	AA	18	18	
Wapke	Stanislaus	BA	17	10	
Wapriski	Lawrence	BA	26	6	
Waraczek	Kazmierz	BA	40	6	3
Warczynsky	Henry	BA	40	6	1
Warga	Joseph	BA	8	6	
Warielewka	Theodore	BA	3	22	
Warminski	Mike	BA	17	15	
Warminski	Stanislaus	BA	17	14	
Warner	Michael	AA	9	1	
Warowsci	Adam	BA	17	5	
Warzinski	Marcin	BA	17	35	
Wasek	Mary	BA	19	29	
Washal	Stefania	BA	19	20	
Washileski	Andrew	AA	8	2	
Wasielewski	Joseph	BA	19	18	
Wasieliski	James	BA	19	7	
Wasiewski	Adam	BA	35	19	
Wasik	Ignacy	BA	18	9.	
Wasilewski	John	BA	8	9	
Wasilumski	Stanislaw	BA	17	37	
Waskiewcki	Teofil	BA	19	11	
Waskiewicz	John	BA	16	9	
Waskiewiz	Monka	BA	4	2	
Wasowicz	Ignacy	BA	18	6	
Waszak	Joseph	BA	40	6	2
Waszkevicz	Vincent	BA	25	6	
Waszkiewitz	Michael	BA	40	6	3
Watahzski	Joseph	BA	16	4	
Watchka	Lizzie	BA	26	14	
Watowski	John	BA	17	4	
Waukowski	William	BA	17	13	
Wawrzymak	Andreas	BA	6	2	
Wawrzymick	Joseph	BA	6	2	
Wayer	Frank	BA	16	8	
Waztowicz	Martin J.	BA	13	9	
Wazuriak	Andrew	BA	15	12	
Wdzrecyny	Stanislaus	BA	17	23	
Web	John	AA	15	7b	
Weber	Anton	BA	18	11	
Weber	Frank	BA	19	25	
Weber	Joseph	BA	25	6	
Weber	R.T.	BA	17	29	
Weber	Thomas A.	BA	8	5	

Last	First	CO	ED	PAG
Weber	Vincent J.	BA	35	19
Wegielska	Agnes	BA	10	24
Weglewicz	Joseph	BA	17	28
Wegrocki	Ramond	BA	18	4
Wegurth	John	BA	15	12
Weilgant	Hattie	BA	19	11
Weiseugk	Michl	BC	68	27
Weiss	Louis F.	BA	9	5
Welapski	Frank	BA	17	10
Welch	Joseph	BC	68	23
Welizcinski	William	BA	16	11
Welkowski	Teoble	BA	9	3
Welzant	Charles W.	BA	18	2
Wendelus	Jan	BA	16	6
Wenedgski	Peter	BA	1	13
Weneski	Ludwig	BA	19	11
Wengielska	Rozalia	BA	15	13
Werczynski	Francis	BA	35	4
Werdowski	Thomas	BA	18	4
Werieski	Theodora	BA	26	15
Werlowski	Adam	BA	35	22
Werner	Helena	AA	14	19a
Weselek	Frank	BA	9	6
Weslowski	Bronslaw	BA	15	9
Wesman	Maryanna	BA	17	28
Wesolek	Joseph W.	BA	1	16
Weszka	Adam	BA	8	7
Wesznewsky	Antoni	AA	18	20
Wewlowska	Michalina	BA	8	9
Weynoski	Joseph	BA	26	19
Wiatrowski	Frank	BA	17	22
Widkoski	Peter	BA	26	6
Wiecinski	Feliska	BA	11	8
Wieczeuski	Joseph	BA	19	13
Wieczkowski	Katherina	BA	18	9
Wieczorek	Martin	BA	19	9
Wieczynski	John	BA	18	9
Wieduszewski	Joseph	BA	25	9
Wieledavitz	Henry	BA	19	11
Wielenski	Francisyka	BA	3	6
Wielgarz	Peter	BA	8	9
Wielgos	Dora	BC	48	8
Wieliesko	John	BC	48	8
Wienerowski	Adalbert	BA	17	35
Wieniszewski	Michael	BA	8	9
Wieprecht	Charles	BA	3	8
Wiergoie	Wiktorya	BA	11	7
Wiesolek	Mikal	BA	2	9
Wiesolowski	Martin	BA	19	31
Wieswski	Geo.	BA	16	5

Last	First	CO	ED	PAG
Wieziotek	Wojciech	BA	17	6
Wighewiz	George	BA	19	20
Wikorski	George	BA	3	2
Wiktorska	Anna	BA	17	16
Wilczynski	Thomas F.	BA	19	24
Wilebski	James	BA	26	4
Wilinski	Thamas	BA	19	6
Wilozek	Pawel	BA	17	18
Wilson	Henry	AA	17	9b
Win	Louis	BA	40	6 6
Wincenty	John	BA	21	4
Winckauski	Stanisla	BA	19	9
Winiecki	Josef	BA	2	13
Winiecki	Stanislaw	BA	17	26
Winiecki	Tomasi	BA	17	37
Winklewsky	John H.	BA	14	2
Winnosky	John	BA	22	17
Winski	John	BA	17	7
Winskia	John	BA	26	7
Winters	Antonia	BA	8	8
Winzenty	Alfred	BA	19	15
Wiprecht	Ludwig	BA	21	7
Wischnehski	Fred	BC	42	11
Wishert	Wisenty	BA	26	15
Wismerski	Mike	BA	1	7
Wisnieski	Walter	BA	16	9
Wisniewska	Agnes	BA	14	14
Wisniewska	Antonina	BA	40	6 3
Wisniewska	Mary	BA	18	9
Wisniewska	Michalina	BA	19	17
Wisniewski	Bernard	BA	25	17
Wisniewski	Frank	BA	9]	26
Wisniewski	Ignacy	BA	2	10
Wisniewski	Joseph	AA	13	3
Wisniewski	Joseph	BA	1	18
Wisniewski	Joseph	BA	19	25
Wisniewski	Lawrence	BA	11	9
Wisniewski	Marion	BA	5	3
Wisniewski	Mary	BA	19	17
Wisniewski	Stanislaus	BA	17	7
Wisocki	Francis	BA	17	31
Wisocky	Antoni	AA	18	20
Wisomatey	Frank	BA	40	612
Wisuski	Amelia	BA	25	7
Wisznevski	Jacob	BA	17	33
Witkofski	Joseph	BA	21	11
Witkowski	Frances	BA	26	19
Witkowsky	Stefan	BA	40	6 4
Witomski	Eva	BA	19	15
Wittkowsky	Frank	BA	9	1

Last	First	CO	ED	PAG
Wizniewski	John	BA	19	13
Wladamcyk	Andrew	BA	19	9
Wleczek	Antoinette	BA	18	13
Wlobkowsky	Frank	BA	40	6 7
Wlodarek	Ignatz	BA	19	22
Wlodarek	Stanislaus	BA	19	24
Woczachowski	Joseph	BA	17	25
Woeblebski	George	BA	25	1
Woechiowski	Joseph	BA	25	7
Woiciech	Joseph	BA	26	4
Wojaich	Strugata	BA	5	17
Wojak	Wladislaw	BA	40	6 3
Wojcheyak	George	BA	19	32
Wojcicchowski	Ignatius	BC	48	11
Wojciechowski	Albert	BA	18	6
Wojciechowski	John	BA	17	19
Wojciechowski	Michael	BA	2	6
Wojciechowski	Peter	BA	26	10
Wojcielauski	Anna	BA	19	11
Wojcik	Franciszek	AA	8	2
Wojcik	Walter	BA	5	22
Wojczynski	Lawrence	BA	16	10
Wojtczak	Marcin	BA	16	6
Wojtiniak	Mary	BA	16	11
Wojtowicz	Maryanna	BA	9	6
Wojtysiak	Joseph	BA	18	17
Wolanski	Edward	BA	35	22
Wold	Stanislaus	BA	19	25
Wolega	John	AA	18	18
Wolenka	Stephia	AA	18	18
Wolflyseak	Peat	BA	14	14
Wolinski	Alexander	BC	48	5
Wolinski	Henry	BA	15	8
Wolinski	James J.	BA	18	6
Wolniewrez	Helen	BA	19	17
Wolski	Francisek	BA	22	14
Wolski	Josef	BA	2	13
Wolski	Leon	BA	22	14
Wolski	Marcin	BA	22	14
Wolter	Andrew	BA	18	12
Wolter	John	BA	18	2
Wolter	Michael	BA	18	22
Wolters	Joseph	BA	18	7
Wonczyk	Tomas	BA	40	6 2
Wonsiewsky	Alexander	BA	40	613
Wonszyk	Anna	BA	40	611
Wontropski	Casmire	BA	21	12
Wontropski	Charles	BA	24	6
Wontrova	John	BA	16	9
Worchezski	James	BA	26	11

Last	First	CO	ED	PAG
Worczonek	John	BA	18	6
Worczynski	William	BA	25	15
Worisnicki	Virginia	BA	19	13
Woroski	Frank	BC	44	17
Worris	Jacob	BC	68	27
Wosinski	Alex	BA	19	8
Woska	Jan	BA	19	31
Wosniak	Bartholomy	BA	17	1
Woushewsky	Stephen	AA	18	9
Wousowicz	John	BA	40	612
Wovakowski	Michael	BA	19	30
Woyciak	Joseph	BA	24	3
Woycke	Michel	BA	17	31
Woycynski	Martin	BA	26	19
Woyczynski	Antony	AA	19	4
Woytych	John B.	AA	5	5
Wozinak	Walter	BA	14	2
Woznak	James	BA	25	15
Wozniak	Albert	BA	7	28
Wozniak	Eva	BA	16	4
Wozny	Leonard	BC	51	12
Wozucki	Josef	BA	19	31
Wroblewski	Joseph	BC	42	11
Wroublewska	Maryanna	BA	17	33
Wujek	Frank	BA	17	15
Wujen	Adam	BA	17	12
Wycesynski	Anthony	BA	19	7
Wydra	Wol	BA	8	5
Wynshowska	Roberta	BA	19	13
Wypracht	Joseph	BA	35	19
Wyrman	John	BA	15	15
Wyrola	William	BA	19	3
Wysankinski	Franz	BA	19	8
Wysokenska	Tekla	BA	18	19
Wystczek	Peter	BA	17	27
Wysveki	Michel	BA	15	13
Wyszalk	Stanislaw	BA	40	611
Wytizsak	Magdalena	BA	17	24
Wyzewski	Joseph	BA	17	24
Wyzkowski	Bernard	BA	17	5
Yablonski	Vincente	BA	17	36
Yakiweski	Victor	BA	27	22
Yakuweski	Annie	BA	17	22
Yamchowski	Peter	BA	17	24
Yancovtz	Frank	BA	8	7
Yankewitz	Stanislaw	BA	17	25
Yankiewicz	Marion	BA	5	14
Yankowski	Stanislaw	BA	17	33
Yanovak	Francis	BA	2	22
Yasek	Joseph	BA	17	23

Last	First	CO	ED	PAG
Yaszensky	Andrew	BA	40	6 1
Yazon	Frederiak W.	BA	19	31
Yegyansky	Gregzos	AA	18	8
Yejenski	Joseph	BA	19	14
Yekubick	Joseph	AA	18	13
Yendraszkiewicz	Frank	BA	40	6 9
Yenkosky	Valentine	AA	18	3
Yenniski	Antone	BA	19	19
Yerhak	Frank	BA	10	11
Yickiski	Michals	BA	19	14
Yokes	James	BA	11	4
Yonat	Stanislaw	BA	40	6 2
Yonavik	Maggie	BA	26	13
Yonka	Henry	AA	13	17b
Yonka	Martin	AA	14	6a
Yonkey	Charley	AA	9	1
Yonkey	Gottlieb	AA	9	5
Yonkey	William T.	AA	9	1
Yonkowicki	James	BA	18	19
Youkin	Frank	BA	2	17
Youkin	Kasimierz	BA	2	17
Youngpriock	John	BC	49	3
Yurek	Fronia	BA	3	43
Yurek	George F.	BA	20	13
Yurek	John	BC	66	15
Yurek	Katie	BA	26	11
Yuromski	Antoine	BA	17	27
Zablotzky	Alexander	BA	40	6 1
Zaborowska	Annie	BA	5	23
Zaccek	Simon	BA	17	27
Zachelska	George	BA	3	9
Zachorski	Edmand	BA	19	3
Zackaruka	Mary	BC	7	19
Zadonoski	Joseph	BA	18	13
Zaezak	Rosalie	BA	3	2
Zajaczkowsky	Frank	BA	8	1
Zaklski	Anton	BA	17	22
Zakrgewski	Vincent	BA	25	4
Zakroewski	Teofil	BA	1	13
Zakrzewska	Frances	BA	25	5
Zalenski	William J.	BA	26	15
Zaliski	Felix	BA	19	3
Zaliski	Michael	BA	19	34
Zaluski	John	BC	68	23
Zamerski	Ignacy	BA	3	2
Zamesky	Felix	BA	3	8
Zametzer	John	BA	3	7
Zaminski	Lawrence	BA	24	11
Zamiski	Thomas	BA	19	1
Zamisky	Michael	BA	40	6 6

Last	First	CO	ED	PAG
Zamoski	Frank	BA	3	22
Zanyzuski	James	BA	26	19
Zapalowicz	Brinslaw	BA	3	9
Zapolowiac	John	BA	8	7
Zaporaski	Henry	BA	8	7
Zarachowicz	Vincent	BA	17	19
Zaralnisky	John	AA	18	13
Zaransky	Josep	BA	40	610
Zarmski	Michael	BA	3	2
Zarnowsky	Frank	BA	40	6 8
Zarnowsky	John	BA	40	6 8
Zaromski	John	BA	8	7
Zarzok	Wince	BA	26	3
Zasada	Vincent	BA	16	8
Zaslowska	August	BA	11	9
Zatrowski	Henry	BA	9	4
Zawadny	Peter	BA	17	1
Zawatsky	John	AA	18	16
Zawieja	Frank	BA	18	15
Zawkoski	Frank	BA	26	14
Zawo	Tekla	BA	40	6 5
Zaworski	George	BA	21	3
Zawut	Valentine	BA	18	8
Zaxarkuw	Philip	AA	16	1b
Zazecky	Boleslaw	AA	18	16
Zbinsky	Anthoney	AA	18	3
Zborowski	Henry	BA	17	25
Zborowski	Martin	BA	17	26
Zborrauski	Mary H.	BA	19	33
Zdanomaz	Joseph	BA	40	6 7
Zeander	Thekla	BA	17	24
Zebroi	Joseph	AA	18	11
Zebroi	Stanislow	AA	18	11
Zebrowski	Wladeslaw	BA	19	31
Zech	John	BA	17	23
Zegulski	Tom	BA	19	35
Zeide	John	BA	17	16
Zelenski	Stanislaus	BC	44	24
Zelenski	Thomas	BA	15	7
Zelensky	John	BA	40	6 9
Zelensky	Julian	BA	40	611
Zelichowski	Cieslaw	BA	17	18
Zelichowski	Joseph	BA	17	18
Zelielesky	Walter	BA	15	9
Zelka	Anthony	AA	18	2
Zellinger	George	BA	3	4
Zendruziak	Yzepan	BA	8	8
Zepkowsky	Ignac	AA	18	9
Zerembic	Maryanna	BA	17	35
Zesiky	George	BC	48	15

Last	First	CO	ED	PAG
Zesza	Marton	BA	3	7
Zewski	Louis	BA	25	9
Zglenichky	Michael	AA	18	6b
Zibulski	Anton	BA	17	22
Zielinski	Frank	BA	5	22
Zielinski	Jacob	BC	51	12
Zielinski	Maciej	BA	5	22
Zielishowsky	Vicenty	BA	40	6 9
Zielska	Maryanna	BA	2	12
Zielski	Frank	BA	8	10
Ziemski	Julian	BA	6	2
Ziendtek	Peter F.	BA	17	33
Zienowicz	Michael	BA	17	15
Zientek	John	BA	40	613
Zientek	Ozbrieto	BA	2	18
Zimkowski	Wladyslaw	BA	17	36
Zimski	James	BA	2	18
Zingailski	Lippert	BA	17	25
Zinkand	Sophia	BA	25	11
Zinsbuskie	Walter	AA	17	12b
Zinski	Anthony	BA	17	33
Zint	John	BC	48	16
Ziomek	Larence	BA	22	11
Ziomek	Wladyslaw	BA	35	22
Ziomek	Wojcich	BA	3	22
Ziornek	Peter	BA	18	17
Ziwowski	Jacob	BA	11	5
Zmudzcijuski	Michal	BA	15	12
Zmudziewski	Jacob	BA	5	14
Zobrski	John	BA	16	4
Zofiezynski	Szczepan	BA	2	6
Zogribci	Wienty	BA	18	19
Zokoski	John	BA	21	3
Zokowski	John	BA	4	1
Zolkowski	John	BA	8	5
Zolkowski	Stanislaw	BA	18	5
Zoloski	Felix	BA	15	14
Zomba	Joseph	BA	26	14
Zomba	Theodore	BA	26	16
Zoranik	Joseph	BA	26	3
Zouristowski	Boleslaus	BA	19	23
Zowodny	George	BA	26	12
Zrochowski	Helen	BA	3	57
Zrochowski	Stephen	BA	26	14
Zubrowska	Michael F.	BA	9	26
Zubrowski	Frank	BA	1	15
Zuchno	Caspar	BA	17	4
Zuchnowski	Stanislaus	BA	17	32
Zuchowski	Joseph	BA	3	7
Zugai	Valentine	BA	25	10

Last	First	CO	ED	PAG
Zukaszewicz	Andrew	BA	35	19
Zukawski	Julian	BA	15	13
Zukski	Thomas	BA	16	12
Zulecki	Ignac	BA	17	6
Zulkowsky	Adam	BA	40	612
Zulkowsky	Joseph	BA	40	611
Zurembski	Stanislaw	BA	17	27
Zurex	Peter	BA	17	4
Zurlesnowski	John	BA	19	24
Zurowski	Adam	BA	6	2
Zwbrowski	John	BA	18	10
Zwooske	Stevan	BA	21	3
Zyba	Pawel	BA	40	6 2
Zych	Joseph	BA	16	11
Zyglarsky	Paul	BA	3	2
Zyglarsky	Powell	BA	16	8
Zyliszynski	Stephen	BA	26	16
Zysk	Franciszek	BA	17	30
Zythowski	Joseph	BA	3	21
Zytowiaki	Roman	BA	17	8